W9-CPZ-870

TOP DOG

Marmaduke at
50

TOP DOG

Marmaduke at
50

by Brad Anderson

Ballantine Books • New York

A Ballantine Book
Published by The Random
House Publishing Group

Copyright © 2003 United Feature Syndicate, Inc.
Jim Davis foreword / Garfield image © Paws, Inc.
All rights reserved

www.ballantinebooks.com
www.comics.com

Library of Congress Cataloging-in-Publication
Data is available from the publisher upon request.

ISBN 0-345-46454-0

Cover design by Derek Walls
Text design by Red Herring Design

Manufactured in the United States of America

First Ballantine Books Edition: November 2003

2 4 6 8 10 9 7 5 3 1

Co

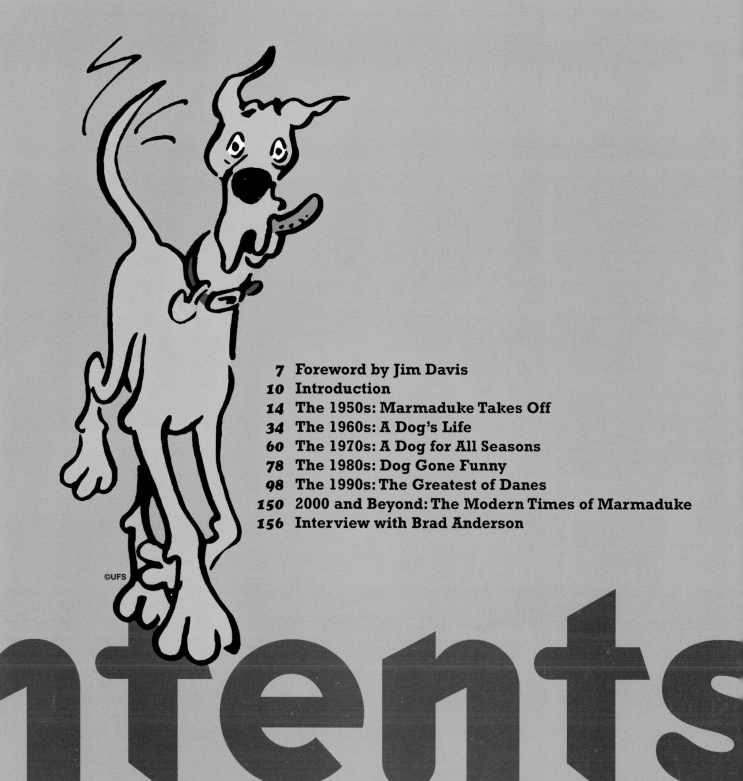

©UFS

ntents

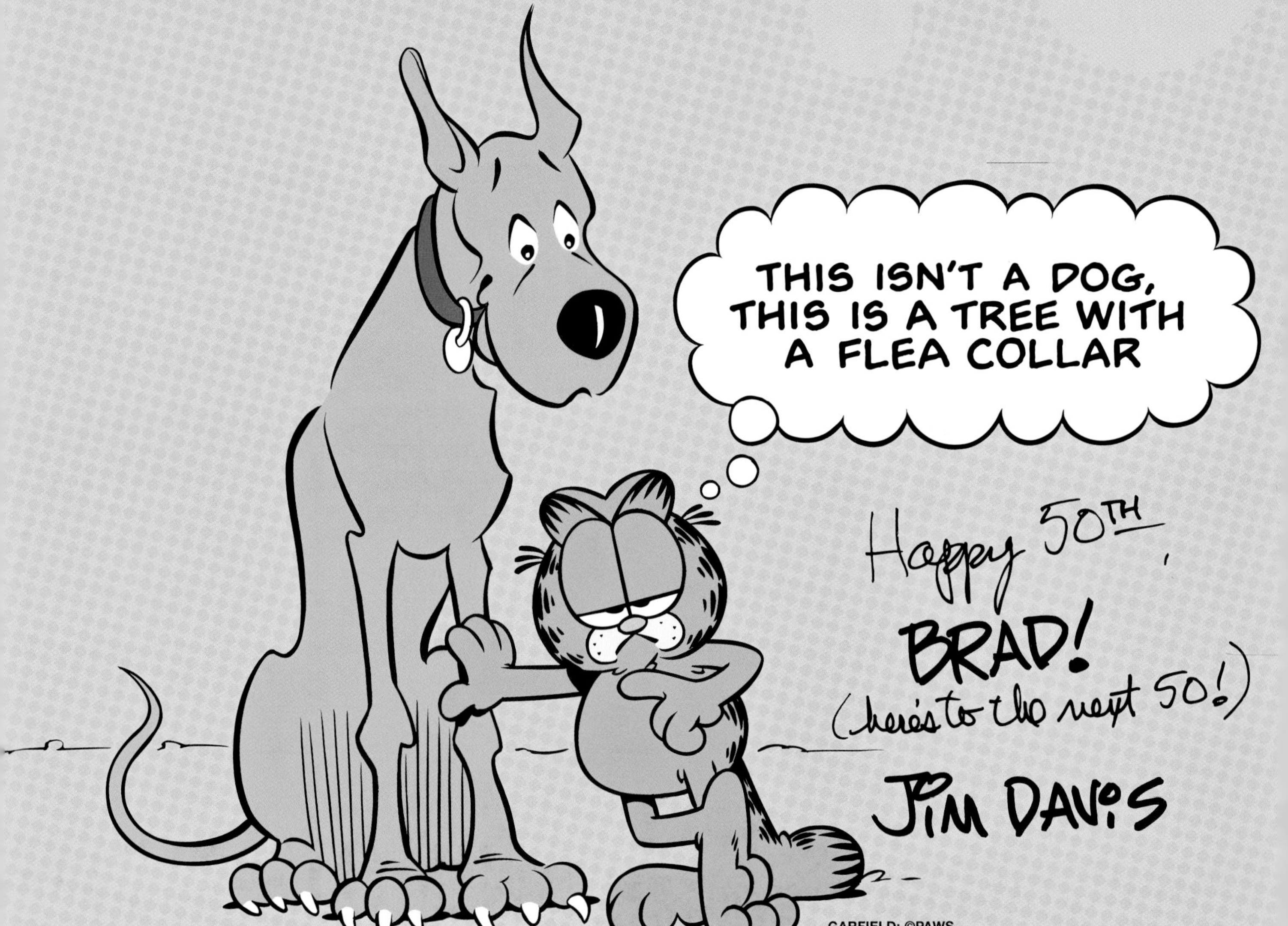
THIS ISN'T A DOG, THIS IS A TREE WITH A FLEA COLLAR
Happy 50TH, BRAD!
(here's to the next 50!)
JIM DAVIS

I'm going to let you in on a secret. Please don't let this get out, but Garfield actually admires Marmaduke. Sure, the dog is embarrassingly exuberant, drools excessively, can't keep his big snout to himself, and makes Odie look downright graceful in comparison, but then there are his good qualities: raiding the cookie jar, stealing the pepperoni pizza, hogging the TV set, and taking over the best chair in the house. Marmaduke is a dog after Garfield's heart.

Brad Anderson understands the relationship between a dog and his family. The Dane wreaks havoc, gets in the way, tears up the yard, and annoys the neighbors, yet the Winslows not only tolerate him, they love him. If that isn't unconditional, I don't know what is.

Several years back, I had a chance to spend some time with Brad and Barbara Anderson. Brad and I worked on a collaborative piece featuring Garfield and Marmaduke for *Family Circle* magazine. Much to my delight, Garfield has come up in Brad's work many times since, and Marmaduke has dropped in on Garfield a few times, too. Brad and Barbara are two of the nicest people I've ever met. Brad is soft-spoken and easygoing and there's always a twinkle in his eye. Though Brad works hard and takes his panel seriously, there's a little boy inside who is having the time of his life. His youthful spirit shines through in his art, too. He literally puts his heart onto the page. Brad's line work is so fluid, it would have to be animated in order to have more motion.

I've enjoyed Brad Anderson's work for many years (okay, fifty, but who's counting?), and along with other comic greats, Charles Schulz and Mort Walker, Brad has demonstrated that if you love drawing funny pictures, and you do it well enough, you get to do it for at least fifty years...and that gives an upstart like me solace.

Here's to the next fifty years, Brad!

—Jim Davis

© 2002 United Feature Syndicate, Inc.

BRAD ANDERSON and MARMADUKE ... and friends!

Dedicated to

DUCHESS

DAZY

MAMA

ALICE EMMA DILLY

GYPSY

Marmaladee

KING TUT

and numerous other animals, fish, reptiles, cats, spiders, and creatures.

They say that every dog has his day, but Marmaduke has had more than 18,000 of them since his first newspaper appearance in 1954—and he's still going strong. But then, why should that be a surprise? Everything about America's favorite Great Dane is super-sized, from his paws to his heart to the laughs he inspires in millions of devoted readers around the world. As *Peanuts* creator Charles Schulz—himself no slouch when it came to cartoon canines—once commented, "Few cartoonists have been able to caricature a dog as well as Brad Anderson with his huge, ungainly, and lovable character."

But Marmaduke didn't leap onto the page as we know him today. Anderson's famous creation has changed with the years. The original Marmaduke wasn't a Great Dane at all. He was a cartoon mutt—a generic-looking dog based on the cartoons Anderson was selling to magazines like the *Saturday Evening Post*. But once Anderson began drawing daily and Sunday newspaper panels and strips, he realized that his new medium required a new style: more dynamic, with prominent blacks and whites to make the cartoons and characters stand out on the page.

Because Marmaduke is a "real" cartoon dog, who doesn't talk or walk about like a furry human, Anderson focused on drawing the dog as an active figure with an expressive face and body language. He increased the dog's size, making him larger and larger in order to take advantage of the humor inherent in an animal as big as a small horse, whose deepest desire is to curl up on his owner's lap!

> *Anderson focused on drawing the dog as an active figure with an expressive face and body language.*

As Marmaduke grew, the readers started identifying him as a Great Dane, and Anderson began drawing him that way. But little did the readers know that the inspiration for Marmaduke's antics came from a boxer named Bruno that had belonged to Anderson's stepfather, and from a succession of dogs and cats that Anderson owned over the years...including a Chihuahua-terrier! Anderson finally got a chance for more direct inspiration when he and his wife were given a Great Dane, Marmaladee, by their daughter. Marmaladee was Anderson's faithful collaborator until her passing some years ago.

All the while, influenced by letters from readers as well as his own observations, Anderson was making Marmaduke more realistic in his behavior, so that the humor of the strip came to be based not only on the dog's excessive size but on situations that readers could recognize and relate to from their own pets. Letters from readers also inspired Anderson to introduce the popular "Dog Gone Funny" feature of the *Marmaduke* strip in the 1970s.

Marmaduke's cartoon family—the Winslows: Dottie and Phil, and their children, Barbara and Billy—has changed over time, but Marmaduke continues to be the star of the strip and the master of the house...at least in his own opinion!

One thing that hasn't changed is Anderson's love of cartooning. He still puts in long hours every day, drawing, inking, and lettering his strips by hand, on the same wooden drawing table given to him by his parents more than sixty years ago. You might say that when it comes to cartooning, Anderson is dogged in his approach!

©UFS

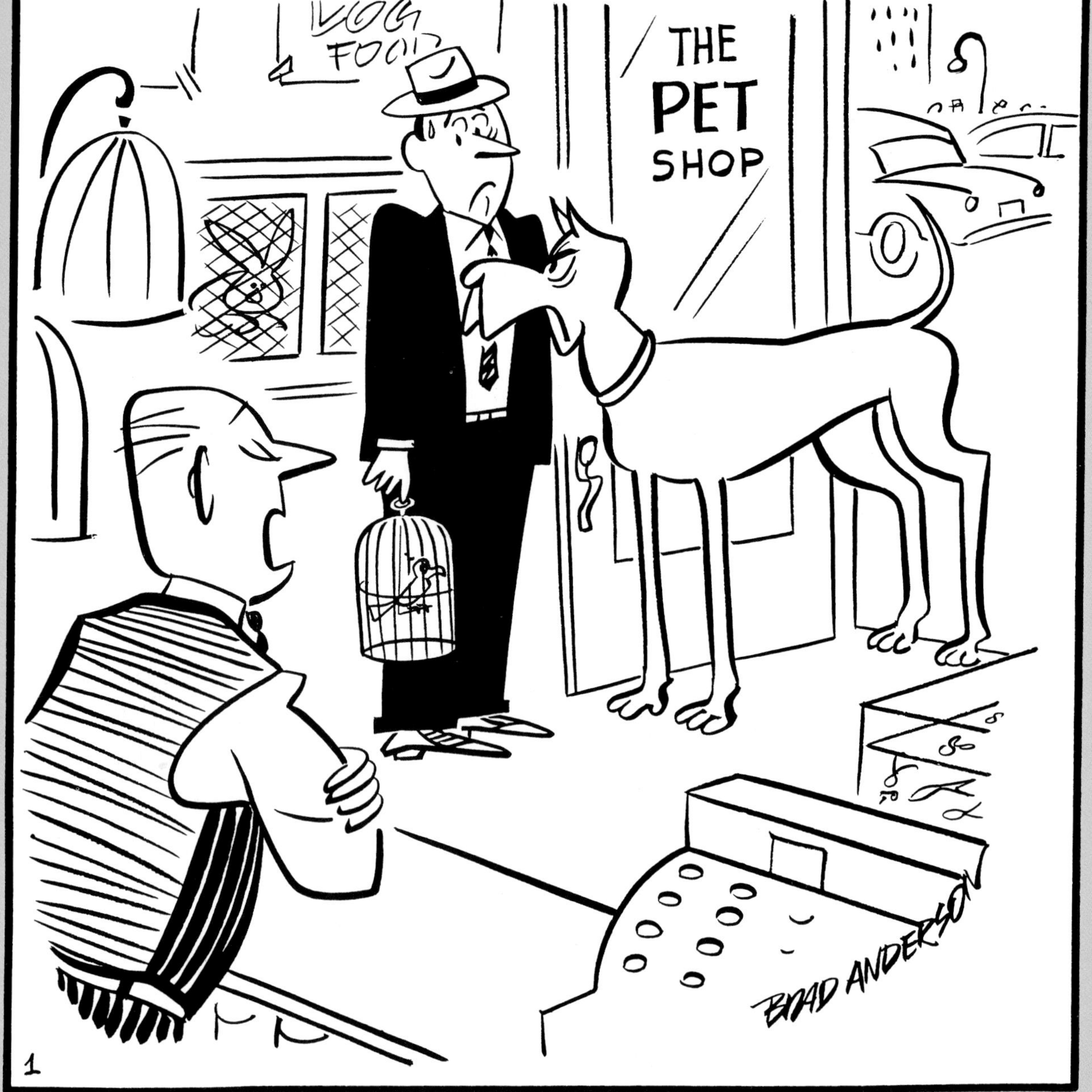
THE
PET
SHOP
BRAD ANDERSON
1

"He wants you to buy him."

Marmaduke began life as a full-size dog that was discovered in a pet store by Phil Winslow.

Phil took Marmaduke home and the daily adventure began. He ruled the neighborhood, shooed away bad guys, befriended the mailman and the next door neighbors, and, in general, took charge of every situation in a humorous way...I hope.

—Brad Anderson

Marmaduke had a real-life model, a boxer named Bruno who lived with my mother and her husband, Del Mabee. Bruno came from Germany, where Del's son, who was serving in the Air Force, had adopted him but was unable to keep him. When Bruno came to live in Jamestown, New York, he thought that all people were his pets, and he loved dragging Del at the end of his leash on some very fast runs. Unfortunately, one day he got off his leash and tried to stare down a locomotive. According to witnesses, he stood on the track barking to the very end.

1950s:
Marmaduke
Takes Off

©UFS

"Good Gravy! What's he done now?"

"Uh-oh! He's had another run-in with
the dog catcher!"

"Hey! Where did Marmaduke go?"

"He took a shortcut home!"

"He's out in the yard. I tied him
to the fence."

"Their baby said his first word
today...Marmaduke."

"Wasn't it nice of Marmaduke to meet you at the bus stop with your umbrella?"

"Gosh, Marmaduke! Can't I even *look*?"

"Maybe they are his favorite slippers.
They're my favorite slippers, *too*!"

"Well, maybe you can ride in the front
seat with Daddy *next* time, honey."

"Marmaduke's hoggin' the sprinkler again!"

"Oh, oh! That's his favorite chair!"

"Doggone it! Does he always have to
be so glad to see us?"

"Chocolate malted...Coke...root
beer...and a T-bone steak, well done."

"You forgot to kiss me goodbye!"

During the first decade there were a variety of art styles. In the beginning Marmaduke resembled a *Saturday Evening Post* cartoon.

The art changed and became bolder, but it still retained the Post influence. The Marmaduke cartoon character initially had an aggressive, frowning look that I felt limited its appeal. I wanted to make the character more sympathetic and more doggy. This required more drawing changes that have continued through the decades.

"Hey! What happened to all the
coconut creams?"

"Burglary insurance?
Are you kidding?"

"This is one time we get to go visiting
without that darned dog!"

"Speak to him—maybe he'll
recognize you!"

"Look, Fred! There goes Marmaduke taking his pet man for a walk!"

"We asked Marmaduke to play cowboy with us...but we thought he was going to be the horse!"

"Madam, he'll just have to make up his mind! He's tried on every coat in the place!"

"Your husband's made a friend!"

"...then I add the whites of three eggs, and..."

"I told you yesterday not to give that *big* dog a bone!"

"Well!"

"I hope *he's* enjoying the view!"

"He wants me to push you."

RUFF

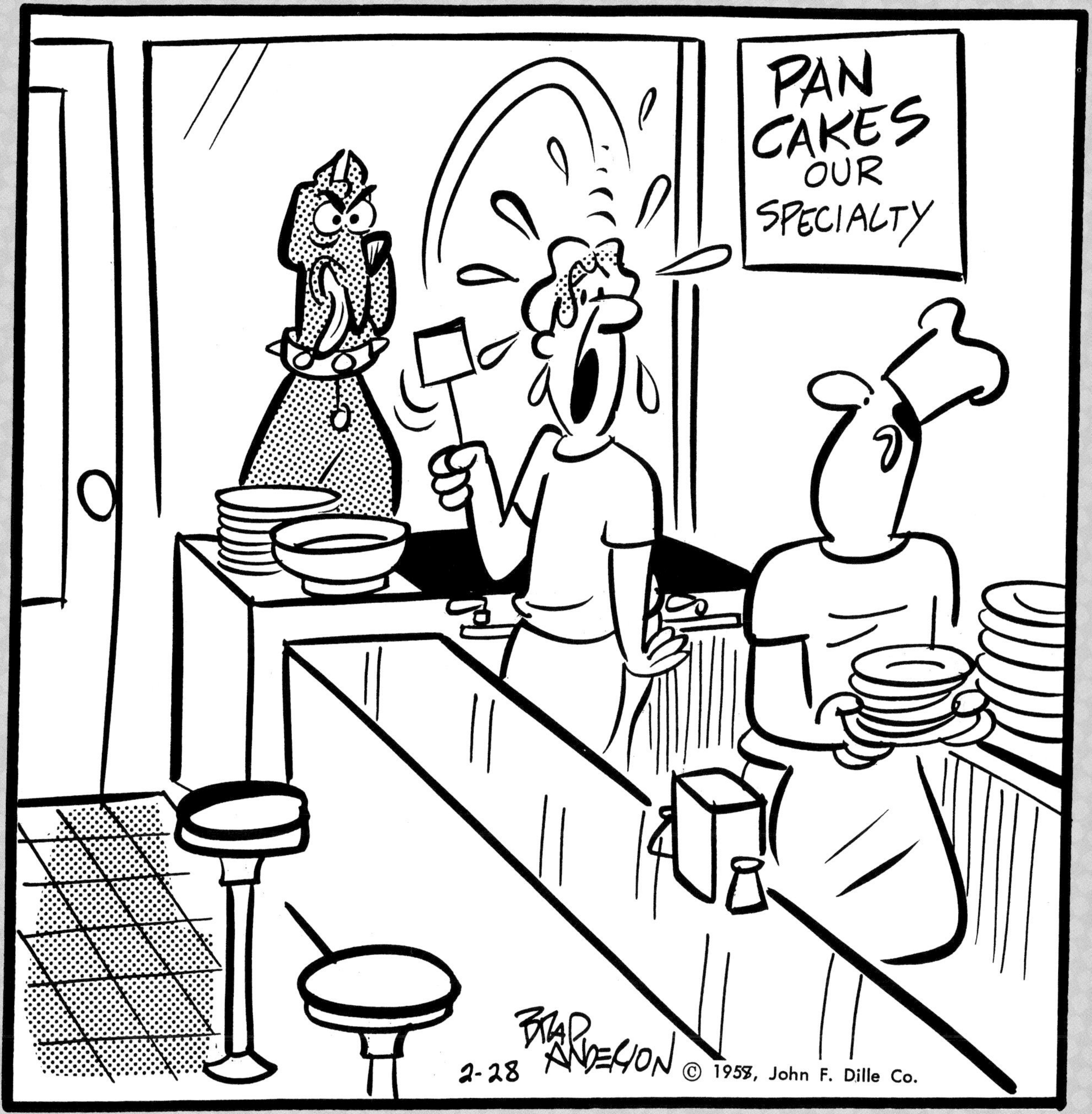
PAN CAKES OUR SPECIALTY
BRAD ANDERSON
2-28
© 1958, John F. Dille Co.

"He's *staring* at me!"

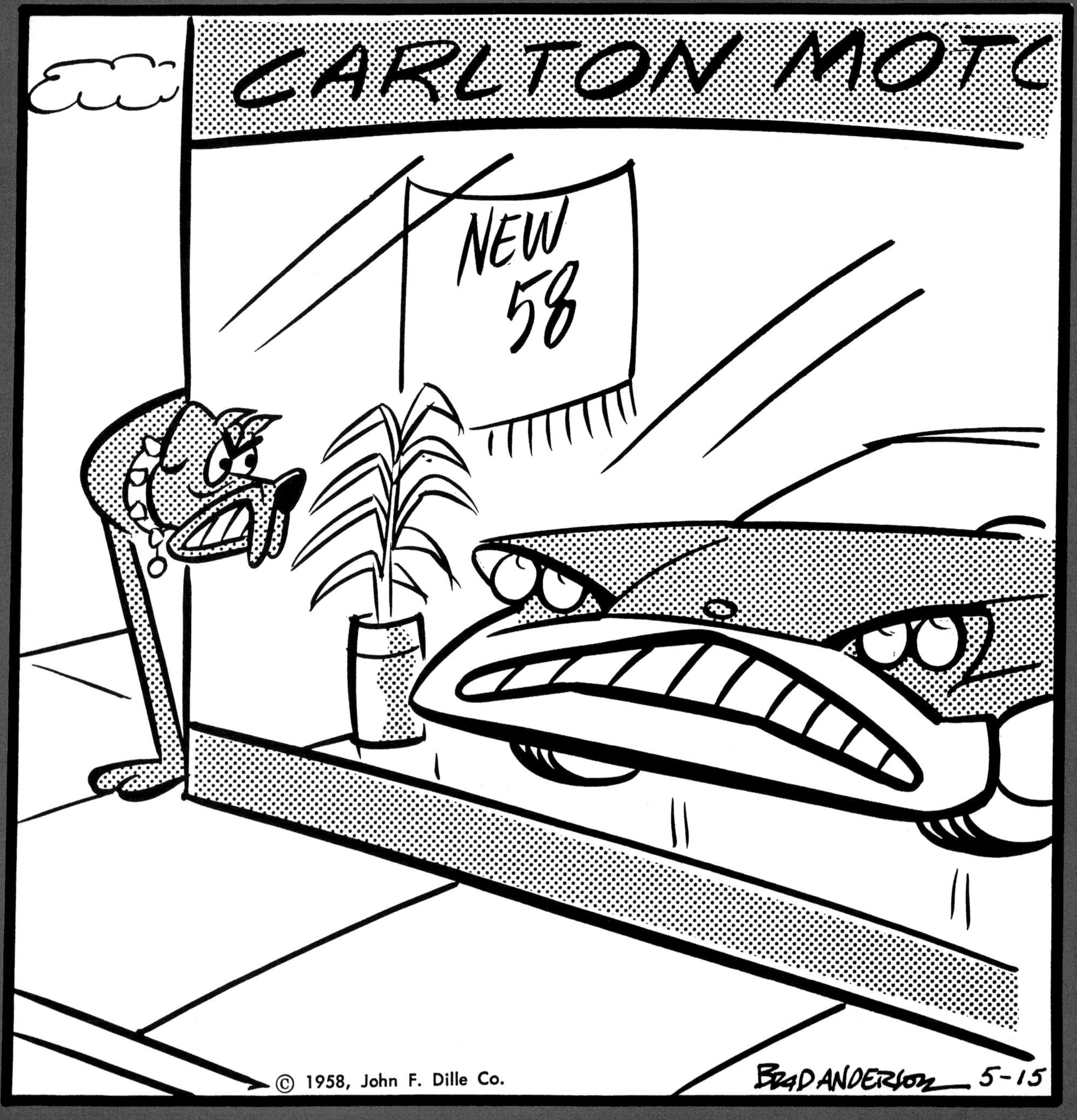

CARLTON MOTC
NEW 58
© 1958, John F. Dille Co.
BRAD ANDERSON 5-15

"PLEASE stop saving my life!"

"My, what a dweat big, adorable doggie-woggie!"

"Let me know how you like this new recipe!"

"Thtick 'em up, thtranger!"

"...er...thanks for waiting!"

"They haven't lost a game all season."

The 1960s

A Dog's Life

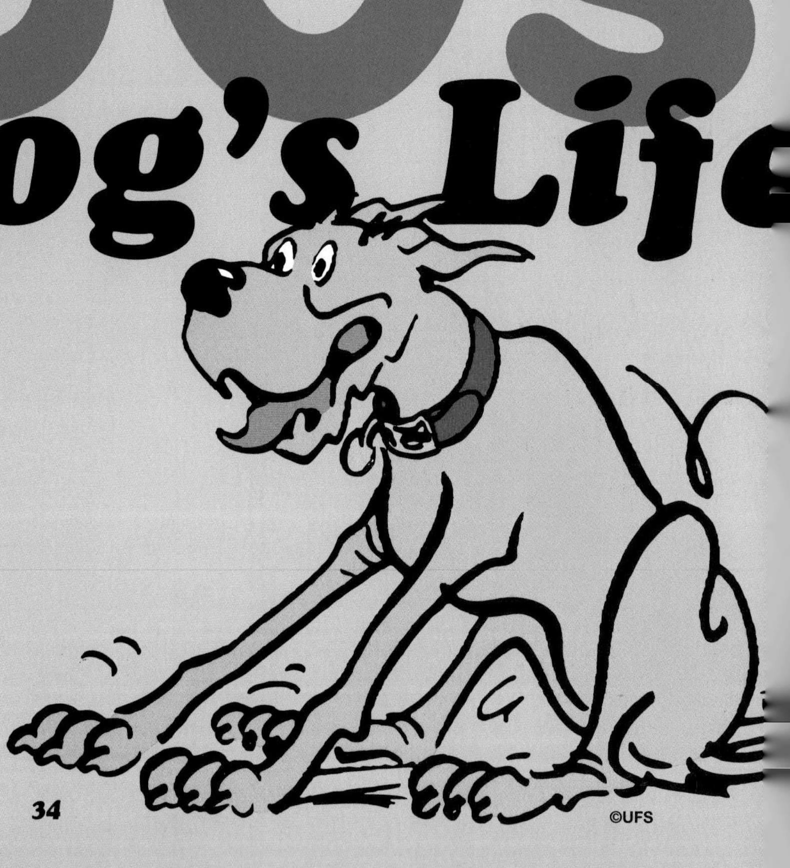

The second decade began to open the gag situation. Marmaduke became a little more expressive and began to appear more visually funny. He gradually started to lose his frown and to show more facial expression and body language. It was during this period that Marmaduke began to increase his number of newspapers substantially. This meant more readers, who wrote letters to me about their dogs.

"They went walking through a winter wonderland."

2-1

BOB ANDERSON

"Come down, Marmaduke! The man
wants to take his train away now."

"For heaven's sake, Dreamboat—
tell him he's forgiven!"

"Don't just stand there! *Punish* him!"

"Poor Marmaduke! He must be out
somewhere in this storm!"

I've been asked if any other cartoons have influenced my work with Marmaduke.

Not to any great degree, although I have admired Ted Key's gag ideas in his Hazel cartoon that ran in the Saturday Evening Post for many years. I greatly admired J. R. Williams's panel cartoons and Sunday strip, Out Our Way. His depictions of the family dog were just hilarious, and I began laughing at his comics as a young child. I also felt influenced by the silent movies of Laurel and Hardy for the way they could create such hilarious sight gags without words.

Sometimes when I'm drawing a Marmaduke cartoon that relies heavily on a funny sight situation, I say to myself, How would Laurel and Hardy have handled this back in the 1920s?

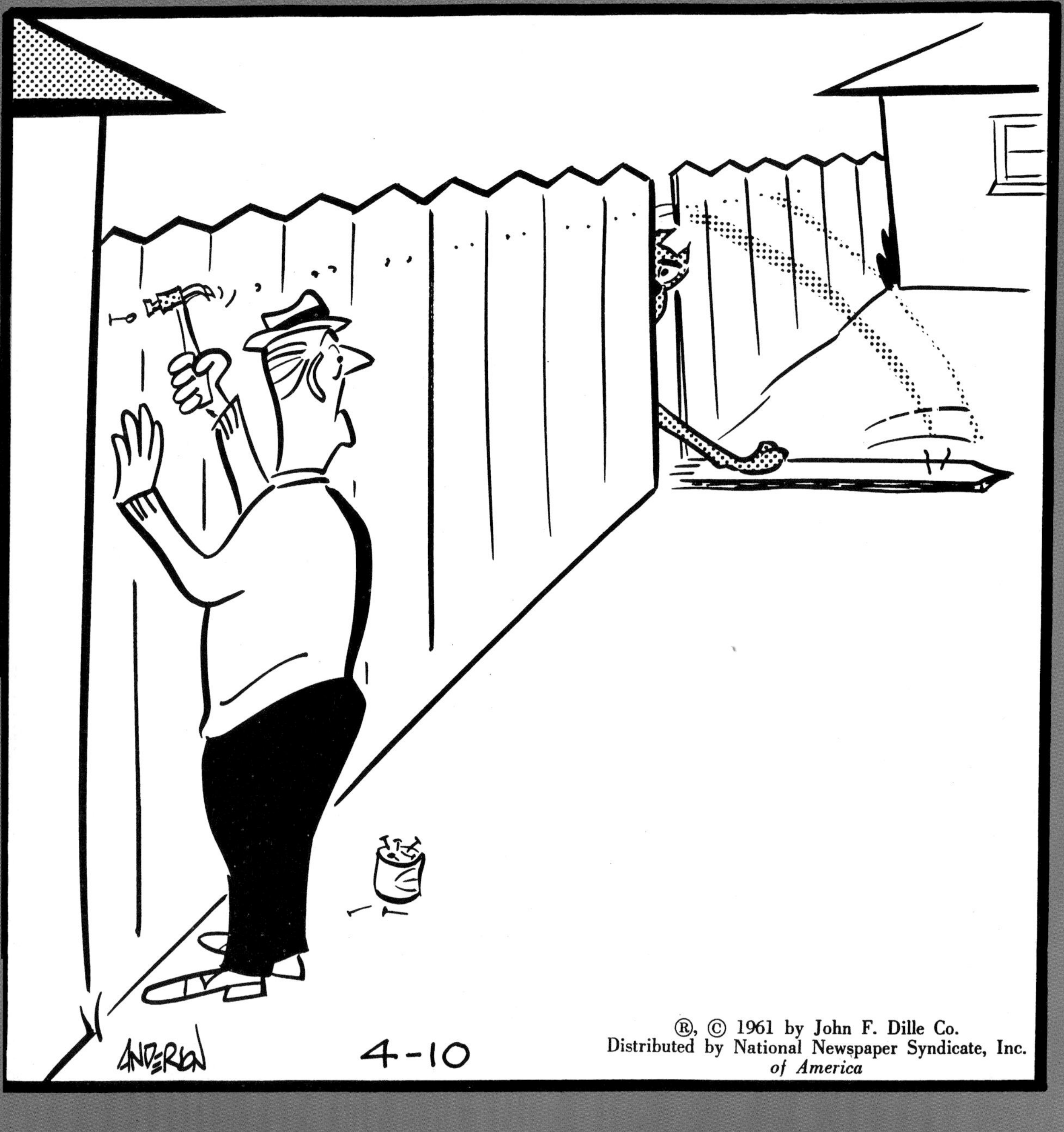
ANDERSON
4-10

"When that dog decides to go...
he GOES!"

"He heard you open your refrigerator
door, ma'am."

"He got tired of playin' wif me!!"

"Now, if we could only find out some
place for *you* to go!"

"There goes the Pied Piper of Maple Street!"

"Marmaduke? Marmaduke who?"

"Something about you seems to fascinate him."

"Satisfied?"

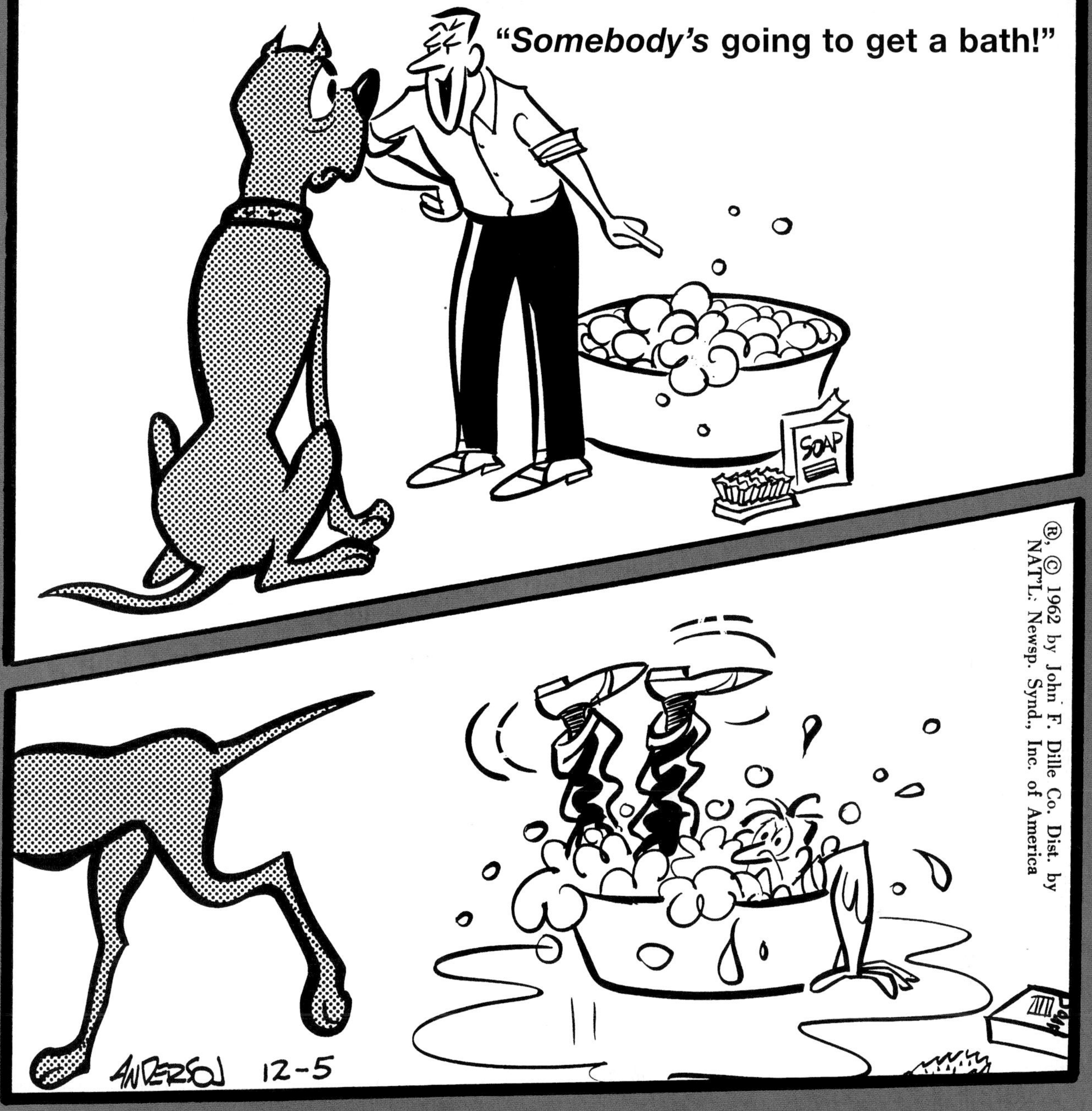
"*Somebody's* going to get a bath!"
SOAP
®, © 1962 by John F. Dille Co. Dist. by NAT'L. Newsp. Synd., Inc. of America
ANDERSON 12-5

"There they go...turning him loose on the unsuspecting world again!"

"You shouldn't have barked at her!"

"We picked some flowers for you,
Mommy!"

"We came for dinner...
He ate ours!"

"Look at that! Just because I wouldn't
buy him top sirloin!"

"What does it need?"

"Thanks, Marmaduke, but *next* time, let
me try to change the ribbon myself!"

"Careful! I think that car ahead is
going to *do* something!"

"Why can't you hate me like dogs
are supposed to?"

"OK...Say 'Woof!' "

"How about a tablecloth, Dottie?"

6-11

"Beat it!"

"It's your favorite dish...FOOD!"

"Better drive on...he still has
10 minutes left on the meter!"

"I'm gonna eat like Marmaduke, so I
won't have to wash MY hands either!"

I've been asked which comes first, the gag line or the picture?

For me it's usually the picture. I sit down and sketch little thumbnail sketches of Marmaduke. Anything from sleeping to flying through the air. This is an idea starter for me. Then I develop a situation and the gag line – or the surprise – falls into place. However, sometimes a funny word or phrase will lead me to a Marmaduke idea.

"If either of us misses, I'll bet we
never see this ball again!"

"Mumps or just a mouth
full of food?!?"

"Now, let's go show Mommy how
you'd look if you were a girl!"

"He must have gotten cold
during the night!"

"Are you quite sure you're comfortable?"

"I don't think you're TRYING to remember where you live!"

"Look at it this way: If it wasn't for Marmaduke, Snyder would never get any exercise!"

"He suddenly looks crestfallen! Was it something I ate?"

"Wouldn't it be easier just to give him a key?"

"I'm getting philosophical about
it...Maybe he'll discover oil someday!"

"Who invited YOU?"

"Somebody to see you!"

"He may not understand the game, but they haven't been able to make a goal in two years!"

"Phil, come right over! I'd like to get something off my chest!"

"Trick or...YEOW!!"

"I've never figured out why they don't
name a hurricane after HIM!!"

During the third decade the drawings became less cartoony. Marmaduke began to resemble a Great Dane. I've never tried to change Marmaduke into a person, although he sometimes thinks he is people, or superior to people. After all, people do such stupid things, like throwing away steak bones or not wanting to share their beds.

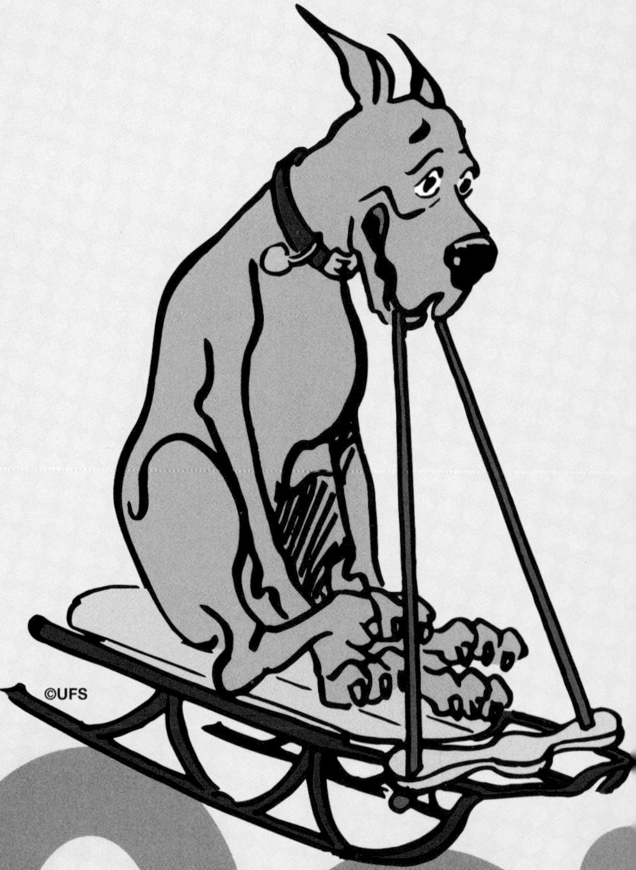
©UFS

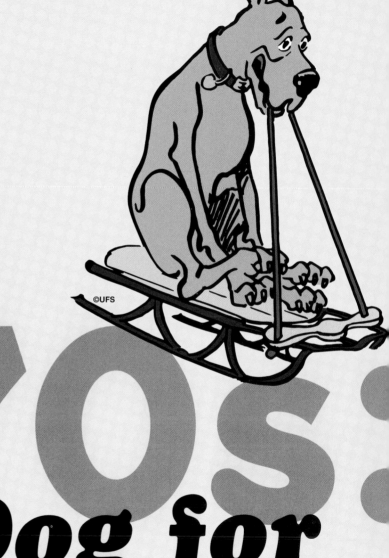

1970s: A Dog for All Seasons

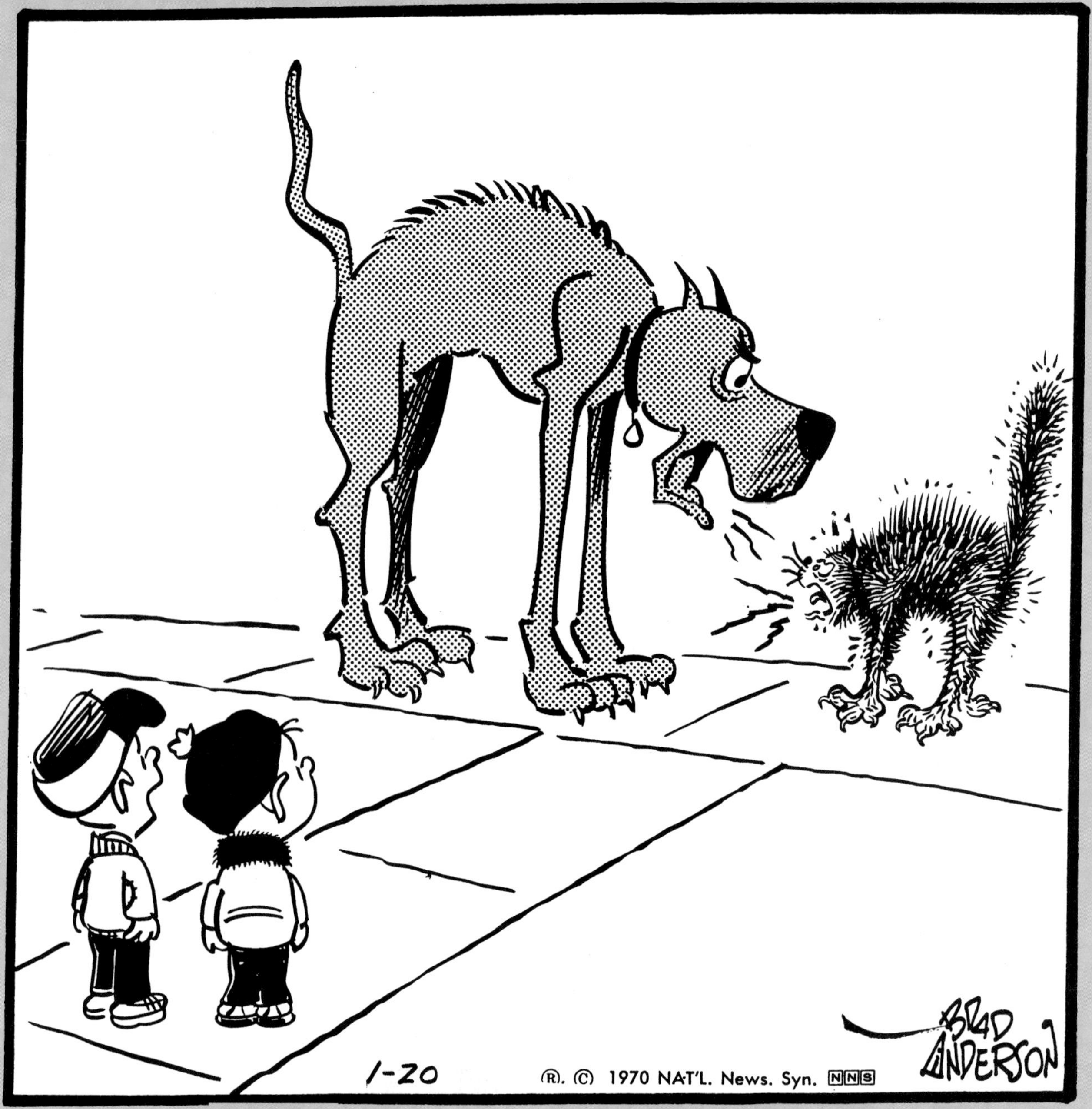
1-20
®. © 1970 NAT'L. News. Syn. NNS
BRAD ANDERSON

"Looks like a standoff!"

"I feel ridiculous when he ESCORTS us through the tougher neighborhoods."

"On the bright side, we may well set a RECORD!"

"I should've told you...that's Marmaduke's chair."

"So, what else is new?"

"He decided to go through
a car wash."

"There's some sort of giant dog
obstructing traffic!"

"OKAY! OKAY! I'M GETTING UP!"

"Try sprinkling hair tonic on his head
and yelling 'next!'"

"I take it he liked my sermon."

"Meow, meow, fsssst! fssst! Sic 'em, Marmaduke, sic 'em!"

"I just solved the mystery of the disappearing pillows."

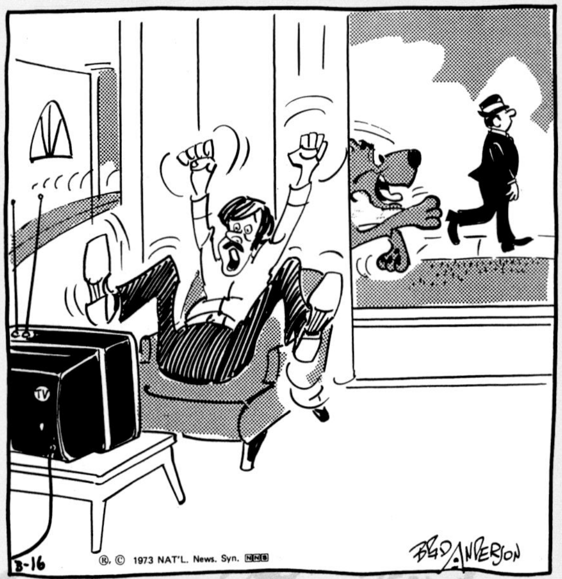
TV
8-16
®, © 1973 NAT'L. News. Syn.
BRAD ANDERSON

"Tackle him! Tackle him! Tackle him!"

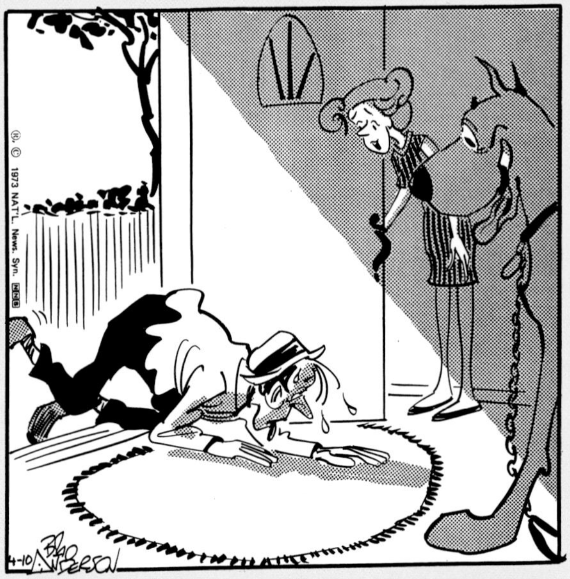
®, © 1973 NAT'L. News. Syn.
4-10
BRAD ANDERSON

"Why, Phil, Marmaduke's been home for half an hour!"

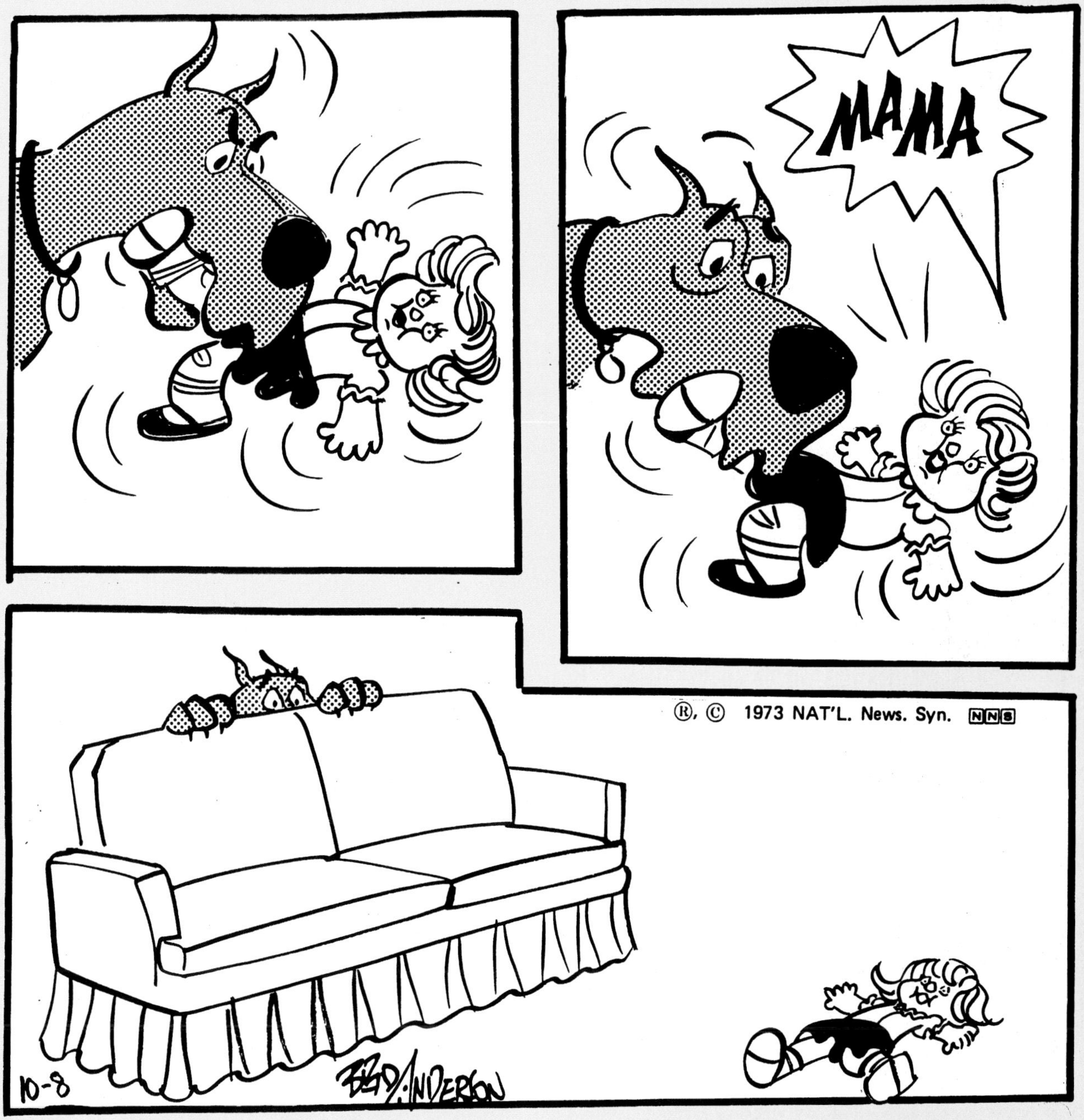
MAMA
®, © 1973 NAT'L. News. Syn. NNS
10-8
BRAD ANDERSON

"This has been a great day! Blue skies, soft summer air and I haven't seen Marmaduke since morning!"

"He's bluffing! He could *never* go on a hunger strike!"

" 'cause I'd rather dance with Marmaduke than some dumb old girl!"

"Those aren't my slippers,
Marmaduke!"

"What is he doing? Surveying
his kingdom?"

"I didn't THINK that sounded like
Phil's usual morning grunt!"

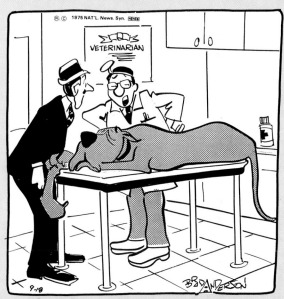

"Sure I can give him a shot to pep
him up, but don't you know when
you've got a good thing?"

Marmaduke doesn't become involved in politics, religion, politically correct situations, or trying to educate. However, I do believe much less harm would come to children if they had a dog.

"Yeah...Ten dogs were entered..."

"You mean, you're jealous of my DOLLY?"

"But, Mom! I wanted to stop playing baby two hours ago!"

"You heard me...DOWN!"

BRAD ANDERSON 7-18

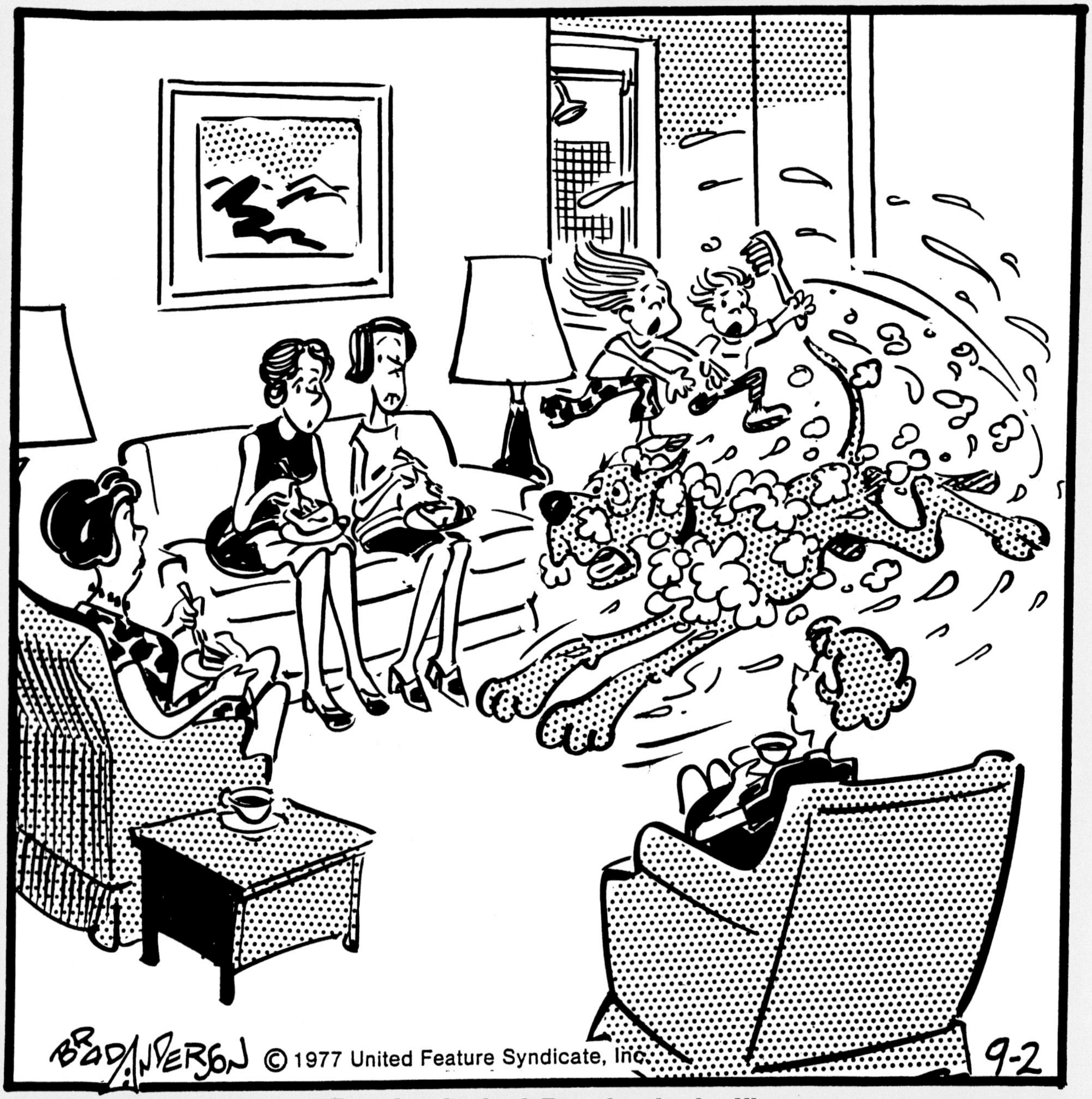
BRAD ANDERSON
© 1977 United Feature Syndicate, Inc.
9-2

"Don't shake! Don't shake!"

"Just think! All the other dogs will be jealous 'cause you'll be so warm!"

"As a matter of fact, we DON'T own a dog!"

"Din..."

"Hey! Those cookies were left for me!"

"HELP!"

"He's part Great Dane and part family."

"Rain, hail, sleet and snow aren't enough...there has to be YOU!"

"Don't you EVER skip school?"

1979 United Feature Syndicate, Inc.

12-5

BRAD ANDERSON

©UFS

The 1980s

Dog Gone

In the last two decades of Marmaduke's cartoon life, he has become much more expressive. I really feel dogs show many feelings, and Marmaduke has been able to express joy, happiness, sadness, and hurt. I don't feel Marmaduke must always produce a belly laugh. He knows a lot of words, such as *Go!*, *Ride!*, *Dinner!*, and so forth, but he can't say them. This gives me an opportunity to convey Marmaduke's reaction...or action...to the words.

Funny

"I had no idea Earth had such a hot, wet, forbidding, hostile environment!"

"She did NOT wink at him!"

"He never met a garbage can he didn't like!"

"Okay, turn the cat loose."

"I learned how to tie bows today!"

"Bad news, Casanova!"

"I wonder what the reigning monarch
wants us to do today?"

"He's gaining on us...I can hear
him breathing!"

"I *am* hurrying!"

"Don't tell me...let me guess...you took
Marmaduke to the vet."

"He's *so* jealous...I have to give
him a squirt, too."

"He saw a bug!"

"I think we have a gas guzzler."

"Remember when you proposed,
you swore nothing would ever
come between us?

"Marmaduke was the bad guy, and
when our posse caught him, he chased
every kid in it home to his mother!"

"Boy! You get *everybody*
in trouble!"

"You owe us two lunches!"

"He stood up just as I was stepping over him."

12-14

© 1984 United Feature Syndicate, Inc.

BRAD ANDERSON

"Divert his attention to the rear,
while I make a frontal spring-
cleaning assault."

"Not now, Marmaduke, not now!"

"Good! Now you know how it feels to
get dragged out of bed!"

"Mr. Rowe stops every day on his
way home from work and gives
Marmaduke a ride."

"Find more kids!"

"Alfred! Look what's in our spa!"

"Let's go back to feuding...
I like you better as an enemy."

"He's progressing nicely with his
commands. He now knows
'eat' and 'sleep'!"

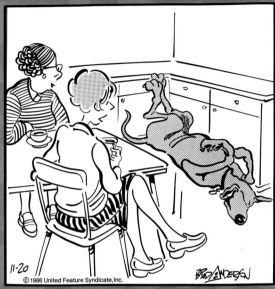

"He likes to start the day out by going to sleep."

"Do I sit and beg by your dog dish?"

"The great outdoors is calling you. Can't you hear it calling?"

"First of all this is not like a game of regular Ping-Pong. The game is trying to get the ball past Marmaduke."

"He's a real problem...he likes *all 36* flavors!"

"Yes, Mrs. Winslow, I *know* you tried to keep him away from school!"

"It's odd...you're the only one of the Winslows who takes taxis."

"Oh, you're a lefty. I thought you were a righty."

"It's him again. That's the problem with automatic doors."

91

"Do we have a dog? *Boy!* Do we have a dog!"

"Repeat after me: 'I will learn to control my tail!'"

"B-E-E-E-E-E-E-E-E-E-E-E-E-E-E-E-E-E-P!"

"I'm looking for my missing teddy bear, and I don't need a password to check your doghouse!"

"You're the only dog I know who can sleep standing up."

"Looks like he's played with
you before!"

"Spare me the innocent look. I don't
have to be Sherlock Holmes to solve
the mystery of the empty butter dish."

"Well, who do we have here...Mr. Mom?"

"Just a moment. I'll let you talk to
someone who handles these
telemarketing calls."

12-26

"I can't believe it...You found a canine dating service?"

"Do you always have to nap in front of the automatic garage door?"

"Don't worry. Even if He makes me a good boy, I'll still get into *some* mischief with you."

"I had a terrible nightmare last night. I dreamed I caught him."

Inspirations for many characters I have used came from my own family: our children and my mother and stepdad. Every construction worker was a caricature of my cousin Sol. I found it wasn't easy to make up characters and names for people in the cartoon, so I decided to use real people I knew in western New York. I could relate to them and it helped to establish the characters.

1990s: The Greatest of Danes

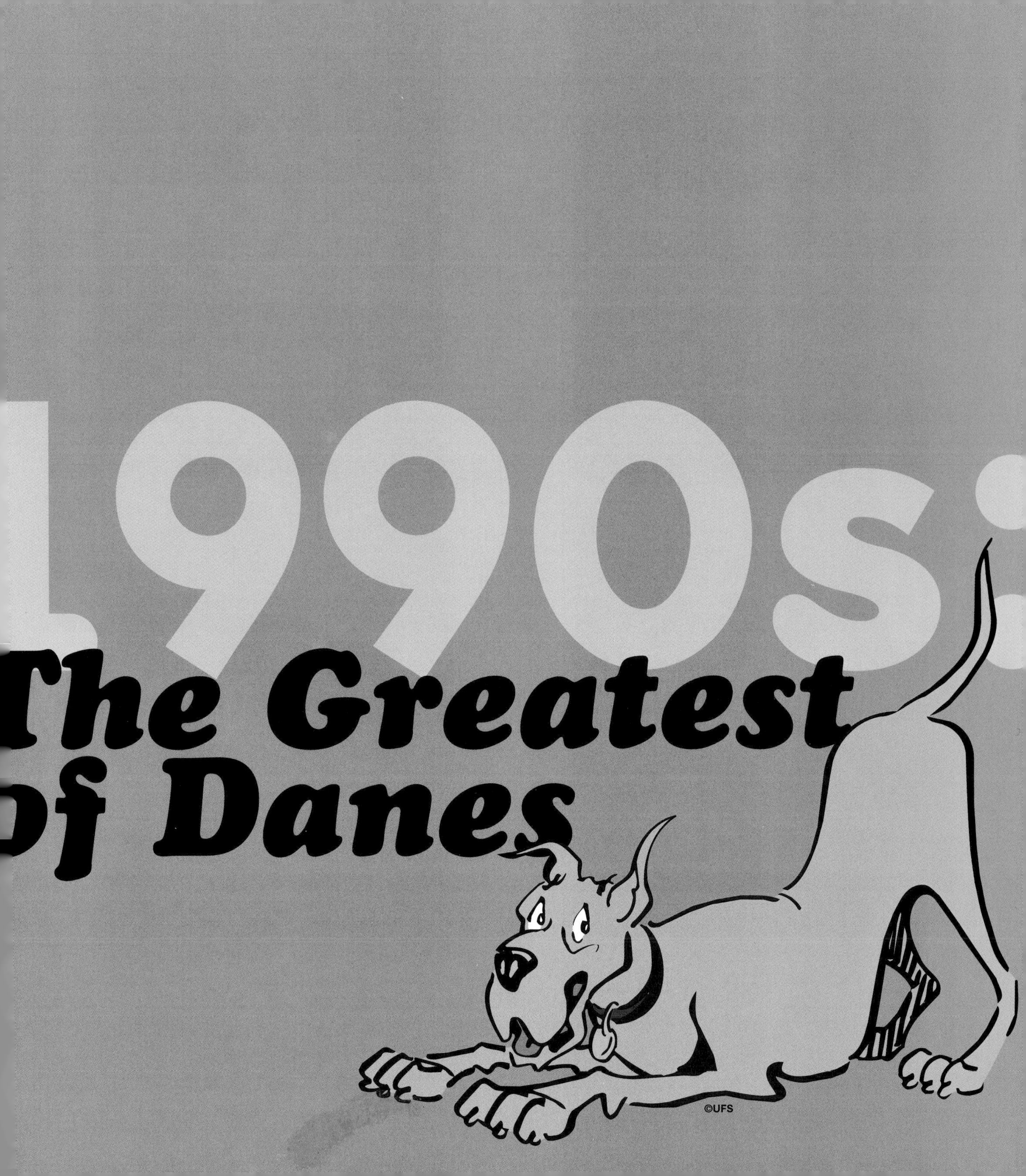

©UFS

"We're each other's best friend."

"Since the kids went back to school, he's right under my feet to make sure I don't go anywhere."

"Well, you can lean on me a little, but remember, I'm fragile."

"Well, *woof! woof!* right back at you!"

"I'm worried. He's running around with a pretty fast crowd."

"How long has this staring contest
been going on?"

"See? You *are* a dog!"

"When Marmaduke yawns,
everybody yawns."

© 1995 United Feature Syndicate, Inc.

"Ahh...it's nice to see a friendly face."

"You mean everyone's lunch is missing?"

"Doesn't that lady look silly
talking to her cat..."

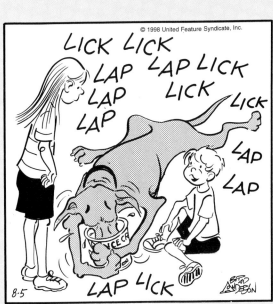

"He's been working on that empty ice
cream carton for a half-hour."

"Aha! He's not so smart.
His lips are moving!"

"Watch. Whichever chair I decide to sit
in will be the one he wants."

"My mistake was smiling at him."

"The kids at school loved him today.
He ate everything in their lunches
they didn't want!"

"Trust me, you don't have to worry
about sun block."

"Well, sure...but you don't have any
homework!"

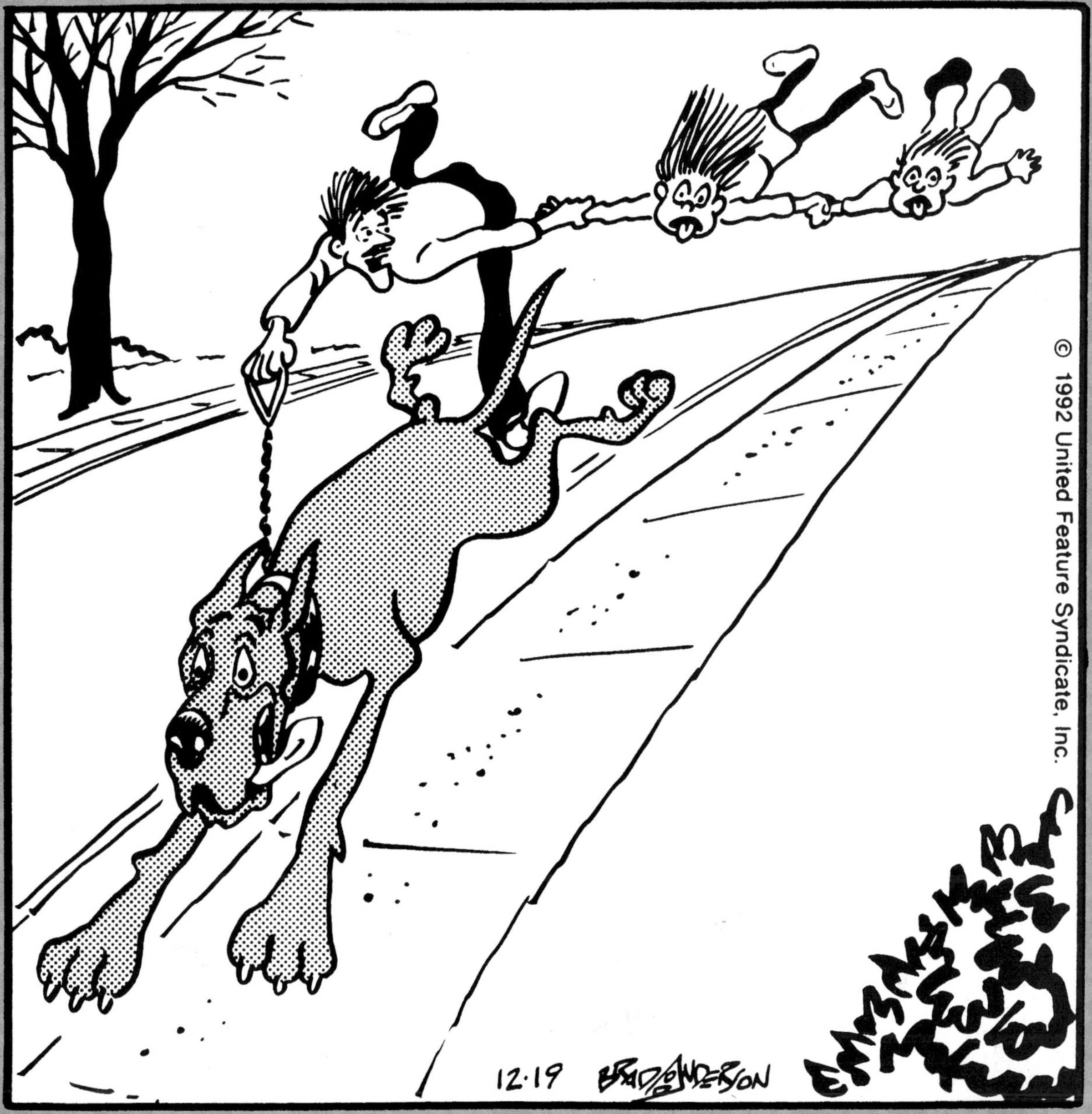
© 1992 United Feature Syndicate, Inc.
12·19 BRAD ANDERSON

“You kids having fun?”

For the most part it's been a two-man show:

me and Marmaduke.

"I'll give you a tip...don't take him
along when you tell it to the judge."

"I think you're taking this man's-
best-friend thing too seriously."

"I hope you have his letter from the
Garfield Fan Club."

"Less talk about animal rights and
more talk about Marmaduke staying
off the couch..."

"Marmaduke thinks he hears the ice cream wagon chimes."

© 1992 United Feature Syndicate, Inc.

"Oh, sure, eh loves it. But just try
to get him to take a bath."

"I'll just take your word that it's
terrible. No need for me to taste it."

"The VCR isn't the place to
hide a bone!"

"This is only a 747. You should see
us when he's a Concorde."

"I'll get the camera. This faithful-
dog-and-master scene may
never happen again."

"Bark when you want to come in.
Screen doors aren't made
for scratching."

"Marmaduke thinks he's spotted
two exactly alike."

"No, he can't sit on my lap and tell me
what he wants for Christmas."

"What good is a remote control when
I can't even see the TV?"

"Hush, Marmaduke. I did
the ordering."

"Is that tail all you're going
to exercise?"

"All right, who ripped the
Garfield strip out?"

"Marmaduke has more petting and pillow
area than most dogs."

9.23

"No wonder everybody was laughing as we drove around town."

"He's still depressed that there's a cat in the White House."

"There's a new family moving in down the street, and they have a dog."

"It's tea for *two*."

"If you slept late *once,* I'm sure you'd like it."

"Marmaduke's motto is 'to each his own.'"

"He's been trying to figure out where the turtle went for over an hour."

"Which one of us is telling this story?"

"I told you not to unfasten your seat belt till we got past the speed bumps!"

"Going for a more sophisticated look?"

"Boy, he seems to know everything I play!"

"Now you're in for it...You left the doggie bag on the counter at the restaurant."

"I can always tell when he wants the comics."

"Now let me get this straight. You were speeding so he could get home in time to watch his cartoon show?"

"Well, at least someone remembered my birthday."

"He's so spoiled! Just because I wouldn't put a slice of lemon in his water dish..."

"Now cut that out! Give me my paper!"

"Maybe if I promise him we'll bring home a doggy bag he'll stop his tantrum."

"Mom, remember that man we passed who was selling balloons?"

"Well, I don't consider it a sign that the seat is reserved!"

"This should be fun! Go ahead, Marmaduke, start running!"

"Why do I let you lead me into temptation?"

"This is our offer-of-a-lifetime expert..."

"He's not a pointer or a setter. He's more of a napper."

The Sunday page is an extension of the panel cartoon where I can build a situation and hopefully surprise the reader in the last panel.

It also allows me to develop fantasy situations, such as flying saucers and aliens, or flying carpets and other out-of-this-world situations. It was during the 1970s that I began adding "Dog Gone Funny" to the Sunday page. I received so many letters from readers who wanted to tell me their dog stories, that I decided to share them with our readers. Later, I dropped the little feature but received so many letters of protest that I reinstated it.

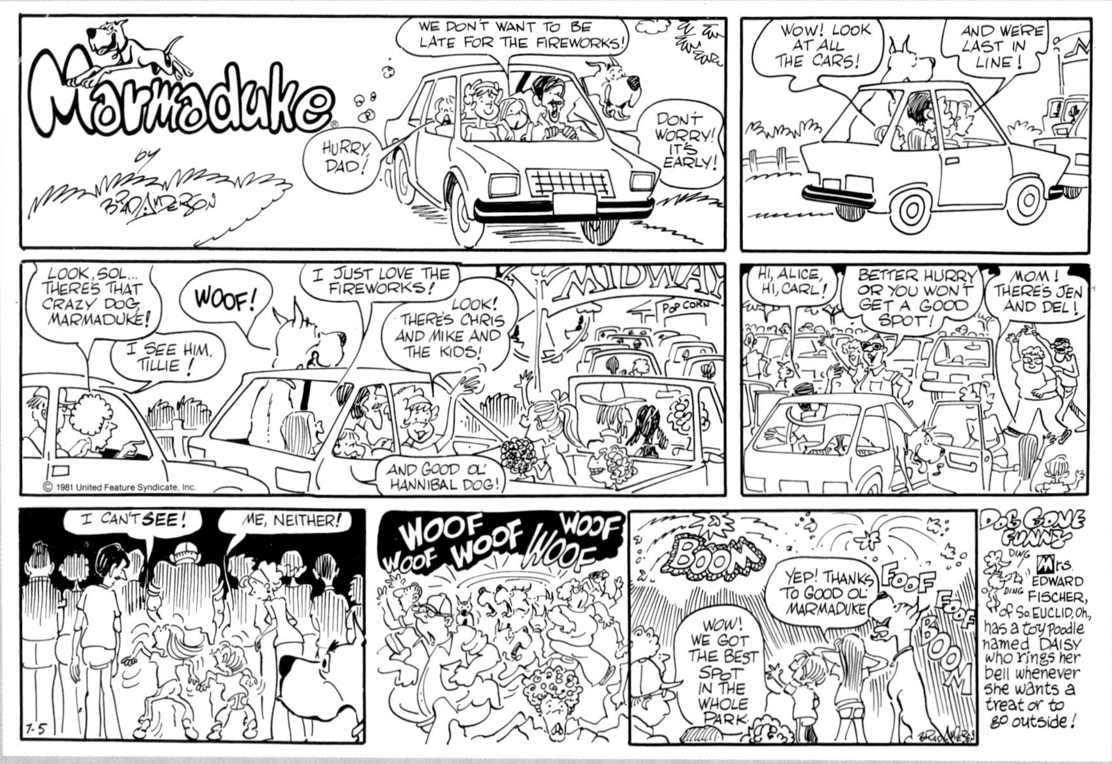
Marmaduke
by
BRAD ANDERSON
WE DON'T WANT TO BE LATE FOR THE FIREWORKS!
HURRY, DAD!
DON'T WORRY! IT'S EARLY!
WOW! LOOK AT ALL THE CARS!
AND WE'RE LAST IN LINE!
LOOK, SOL... THERE'S THAT CRAZY DOG, MARMADUKE!
I SEE HIM, TILLIE!
WOOF!
I JUST LOVE THE FIREWORKS!
LOOK! THERE'S CHRIS AND MIKE AND THE KIDS!
AND GOOD OL' HANNIBAL DOG!
MIDWAY
POP CORN
© 1981 United Feature Syndicate, Inc.
HI, ALICE, HI, CARL!
BETTER HURRY OR YOU WON'T GET A GOOD SPOT!
MOM! THERE'S JEN AND DEL!
I CAN'T SEE!
ME, NEITHER!
7-5
WOOF WOOF WOOF WOOF WOOF
BOOM
YEP! THANKS TO GOOD OL' MARMADUKE!
FOOF
FOOF
BOOM
WOW! WE GOT THE BEST SPOT IN THE WHOLE PARK!
DOG GONE FUNNY
DING
DING
Mrs. EDWARD FISCHER, of So. EUCLID, Oh, has a toy Poodle named DAISY who rings her bell whenever she wants a treat or to go outside!

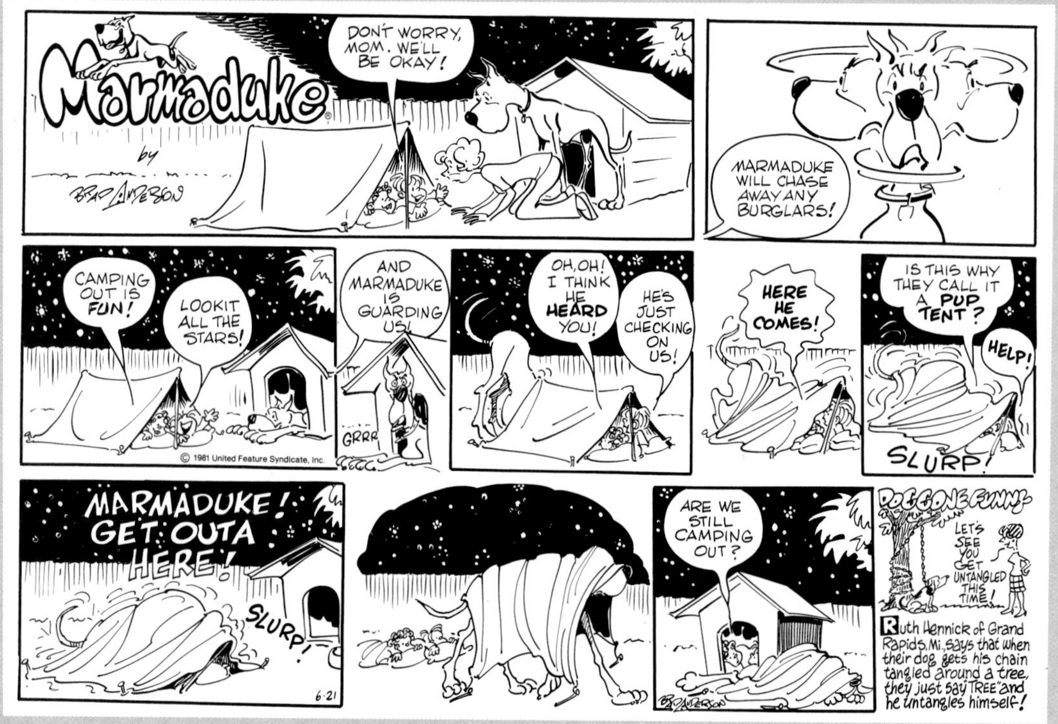
Marmaduke
by
BRAD ANDERSON
DON'T WORRY, MOM. WE'LL BE OKAY!
MARMADUKE WILL CHASE AWAY ANY BURGLARS!
CAMPING OUT IS FUN!
LOOKIT ALL THE STARS!
© 1981 United Feature Syndicate, Inc.
AND MARMADUKE IS GUARDING US!
GRRR
OH, OH! I THINK HE HEARD YOU!
HE'S JUST CHECKING ON US!
HERE HE COMES!
IS THIS WHY THEY CALL IT A PUP TENT?
HELP!
SLURP!
MARMADUKE! GET OUTA HERE!
SLURP!
6-21
ARE WE STILL CAMPING OUT?
DOG GONE FUNNY
LET'S SEE YOU GET UNTANGLED THIS TIME!
Ruth Hennick of Grand Rapids, Mi., says that when their dog gets his chain tangled around a tree, they just say 'TREE' and he untangles himself!

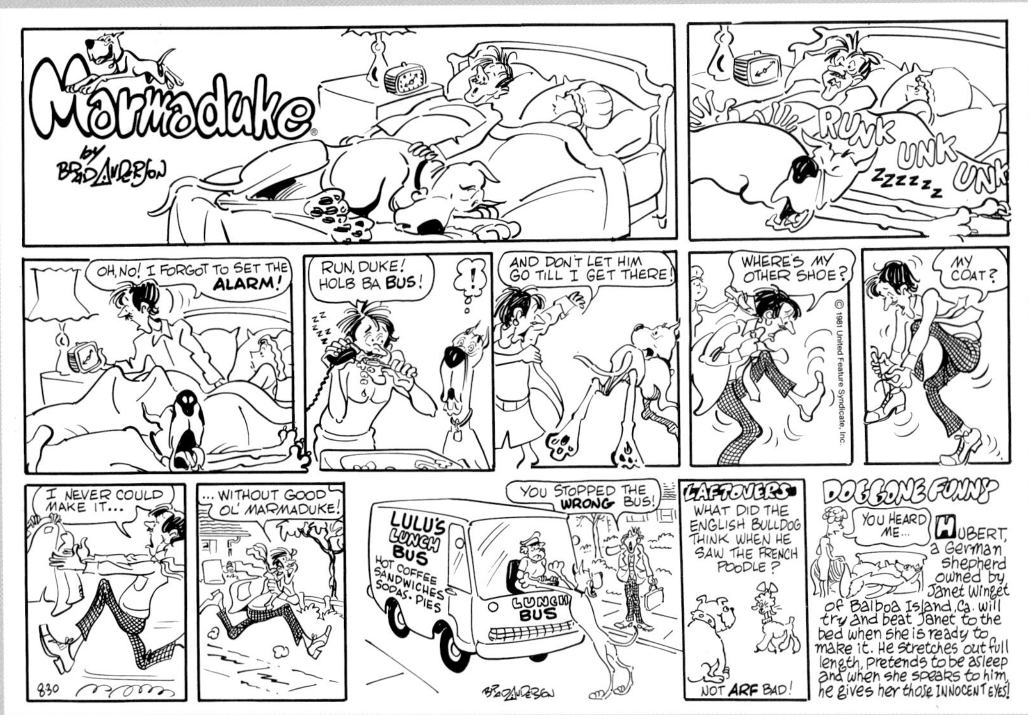
Marmaduke
by BRAD ANDERSON
RUNK UNK UNK
ZZZZZZ
OH, NO! I FORGOT TO SET THE ALARM!
RUN, DUKE! HOLB BA BUS!
AND DON'T LET HIM GO TILL I GET THERE!
WHERE'S MY OTHER SHOE?
© 1981 United Feature Syndicate, Inc.
MY COAT?
I NEVER COULD MAKE IT...
...WITHOUT GOOD OL' MARMADUKE!
8-30
LULU'S LUNCH BUS
HOT COFFEE SANDWICHES SODAS. PIES
LUNCH BUS
YOU STOPPED THE WRONG BUS!
BRAD ANDERSON
LAFTOVERS
WHAT DID THE ENGLISH BULLDOG THINK WHEN HE SAW THE FRENCH POODLE?
NOT ARF BAD!
DOG GONE FUNNY
YOU HEARD ME...
HUBERT, a German shepherd owned by Janet Winget of Balboa Island, Ca. will try and beat Janet to the bed when she is ready to make it. He stretches out full length, pretends to be asleep and when she speaks to him, he gives her those INNOCENT EYES!

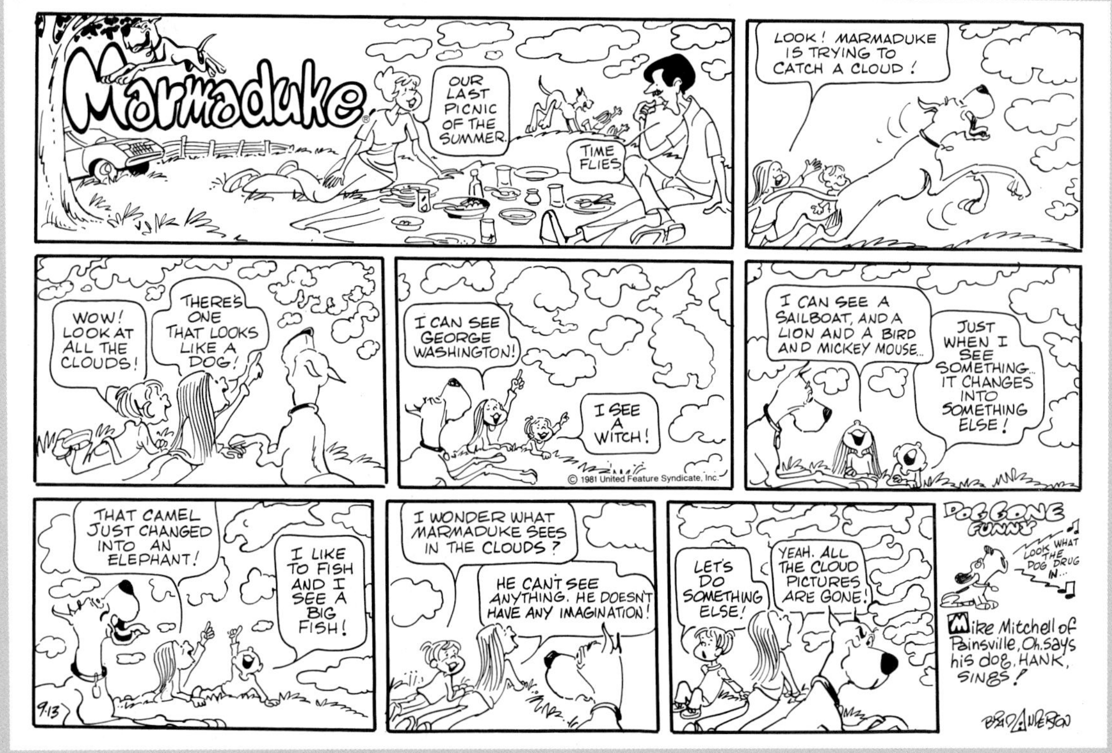
Marmaduke
OUR LAST PICNIC OF THE SUMMER.
TIME FLIES.
LOOK! MARMADUKE IS TRYING TO CATCH A CLOUD!
WOW! LOOK AT ALL THE CLOUDS!
THERE'S ONE THAT LOOKS LIKE A DOG!
I CAN SEE GEORGE WASHINGTON!
I SEE A WITCH!
© 1981 United Feature Syndicate, Inc.
I CAN SEE A SAILBOAT, AND A LION AND A BIRD AND MICKEY MOUSE...
JUST WHEN I SEE SOMETHING... IT CHANGES INTO SOMETHING ELSE!
THAT CAMEL JUST CHANGED INTO AN ELEPHANT!
I LIKE TO FISH AND I SEE A BIG FISH!
9-13
I WONDER WHAT MARMADUKE SEES IN THE CLOUDS?
HE CAN'T SEE ANYTHING. HE DOESN'T HAVE ANY IMAGINATION!
LET'S DO SOMETHING ELSE!
YEAH. ALL THE CLOUD PICTURES ARE GONE!
DOG GONE FUNNY
LOOK WHAT THE DOG DRUG IN...
Mike Mitchell of Painsville, Oh. says his dog, HANK, sings!
BRAD ANDERSON

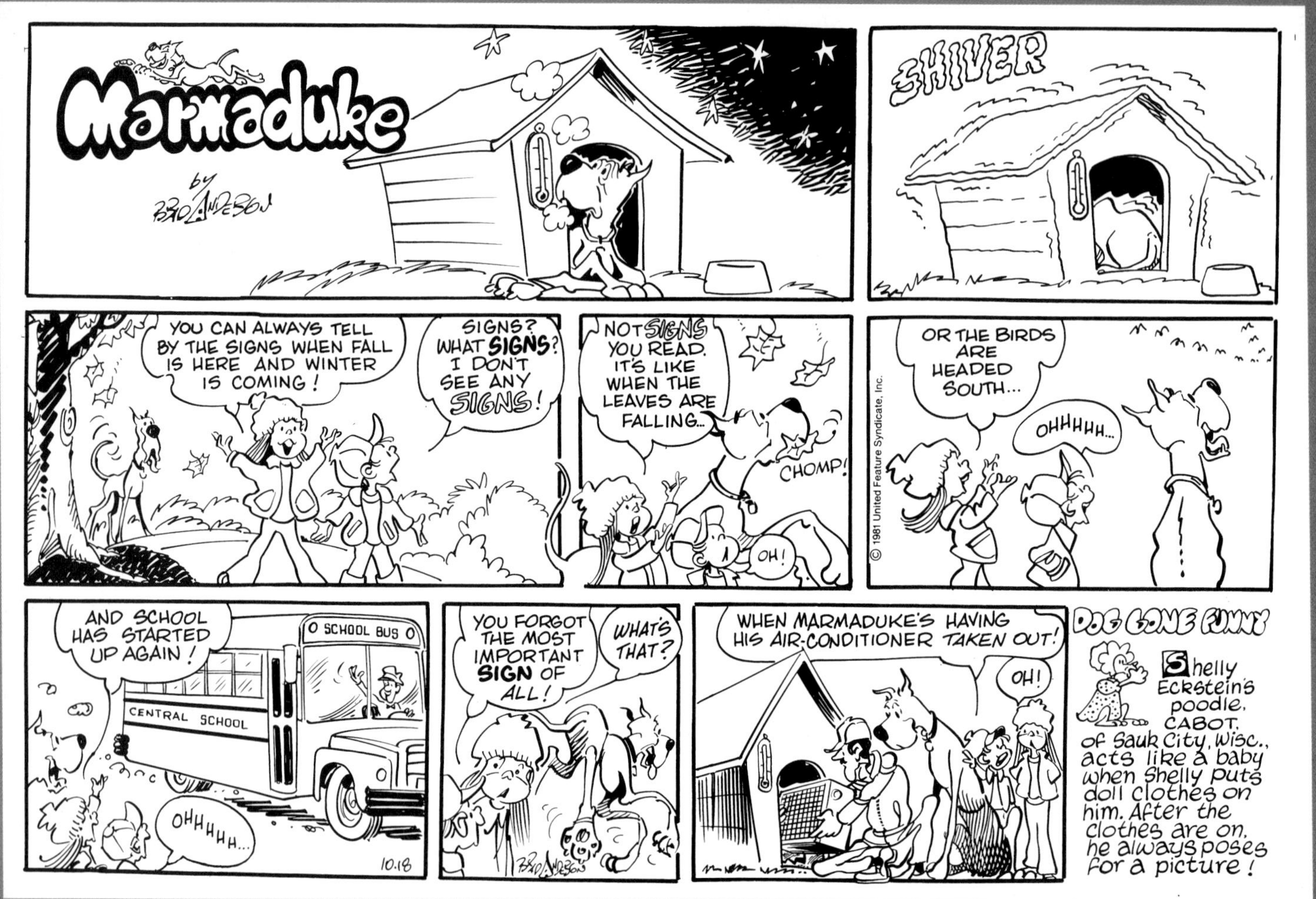
Marmaduke
by Brad Anderson
SHIVER
YOU CAN ALWAYS TELL BY THE SIGNS WHEN FALL IS HERE AND WINTER IS COMING!
SIGNS? WHAT SIGNS? I DON'T SEE ANY SIGNS!
NOT SIGNS YOU READ. IT'S LIKE WHEN THE LEAVES ARE FALLING...
CHOMP!
OH!
OR THE BIRDS ARE HEADED SOUTH...
OHHHHH...
© 1981 United Feature Syndicate, Inc.
AND SCHOOL HAS STARTED UP AGAIN!
SCHOOL BUS
CENTRAL SCHOOL
OHHHHH...
10.18
YOU FORGOT THE MOST IMPORTANT SIGN OF ALL!
WHAT'S THAT?
WHEN MARMADUKE'S HAVING HIS AIR-CONDITIONER TAKEN OUT!
OH!
DOG GONE FUNNY
Shelly Eckstein's poodle, CABOT, of Sauk City, Wisc., acts like a baby when Shelly puts doll clothes on him. After the clothes are on, he always poses for a picture!

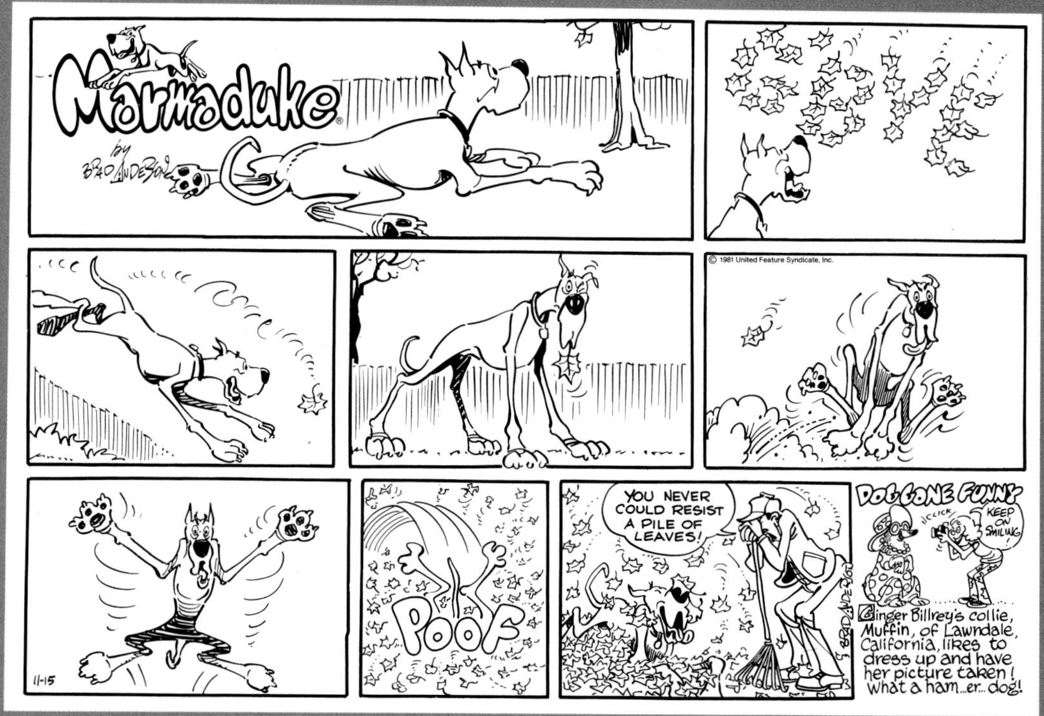
Marmaduke
by
BRAD ANDERSON
© 1981 United Feature Syndicate, Inc.
11-15
POOF
YOU NEVER COULD RESIST A PILE OF LEAVES!
DOG GONE FUNNY
KEEP ON SMILING!
Ginger Billrey's collie, Muffin, of Lawndale, California, likes to dress up and have her picture taken! What a ham...er...dog!

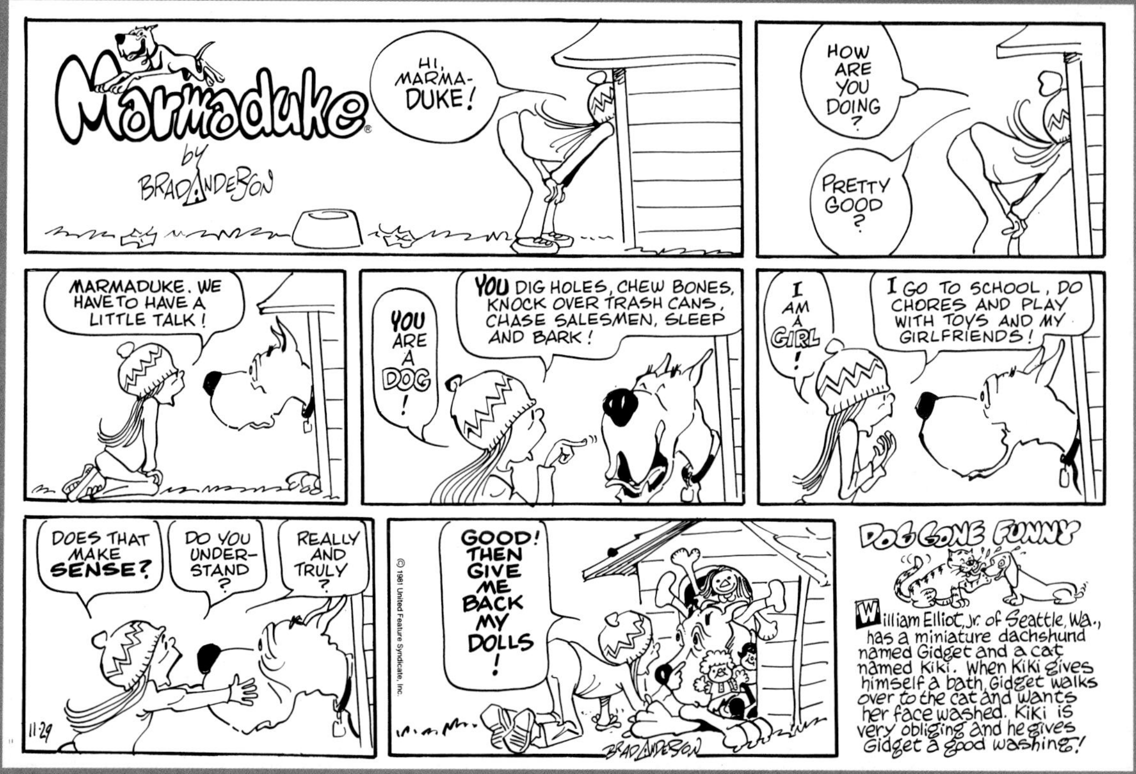
Marmaduke
by
BRAD ANDERSON
HI, MARMA-DUKE!
HOW ARE YOU DOING?
PRETTY GOOD?
MARMADUKE. WE HAVE TO HAVE A LITTLE TALK!
YOU ARE A DOG!
YOU DIG HOLES, CHEW BONES, KNOCK OVER TRASH CANS, CHASE SALESMEN, SLEEP AND BARK!
I AM A GIRL!
I GO TO SCHOOL, DO CHORES AND PLAY WITH TOYS AND MY GIRLFRIENDS!
DOES THAT MAKE SENSE?
DO YOU UNDERSTAND?
REALLY AND TRULY?
11-29
© 1981 United Feature Syndicate, Inc.
GOOD! THEN GIVE ME BACK MY DOLLS!
DOG GONE FUNNY
William Elliot, Jr. of Seattle, Wa., has a miniature dachshund named Gidget and a cat named Kiki. When Kiki gives himself a bath, Gidget walks over to the cat and wants her face washed. Kiki is very obliging and he gives Gidget a good washing!

In today's market there are far fewer newspapers. In times past almost every city had a morning and an afternoon paper.

Now there is usually only one morning paper, and it carries all the comics that formerly appeared in tow or in other papers in that market.

Consequently, comics have shrunk in size to accommodate the increased number on a page. Marmaduke is very large and lacks cuteness, but I try to make him as large as possible in each panel. So if my Sunday page must be shrunk to a very small size, it's my hope that the artwork will still pop off the page.

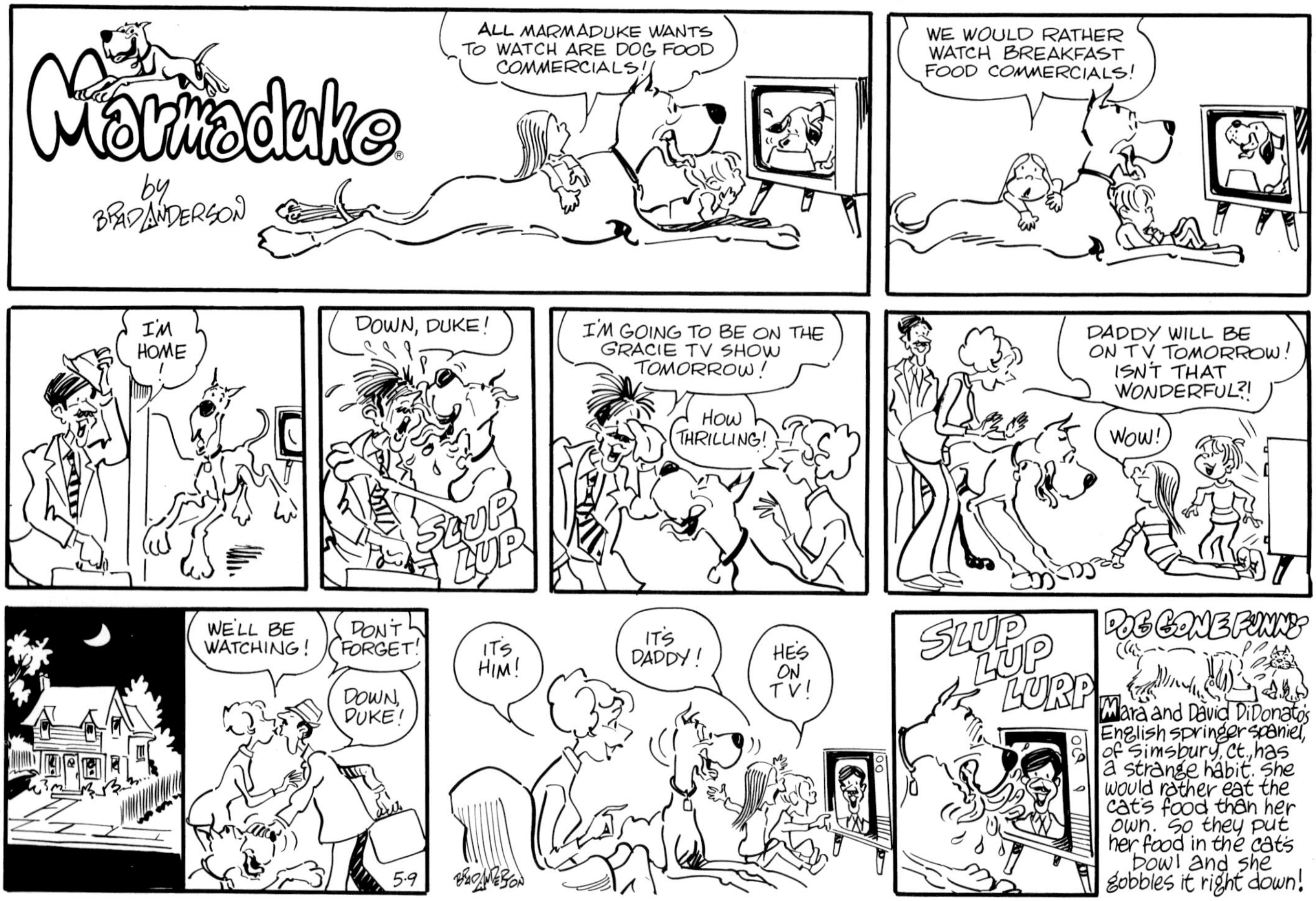
Marmaduke
by BRAD ANDERSON
ALL MARMADUKE WANTS TO WATCH ARE DOG FOOD COMMERCIALS!
WE WOULD RATHER WATCH BREAKFAST FOOD COMMERCIALS!
I'M HOME!
DOWN, DUKE!
SLUP LUP
I'M GOING TO BE ON THE GRACIE TV SHOW TOMORROW!
HOW THRILLING!
DADDY WILL BE ON TV TOMORROW! ISN'T THAT WONDERFUL?!
WOW!
WE'LL BE WATCHING!
DON'T FORGET!
DOWN, DUKE!
5-9
IT'S HIM!
IT'S DADDY!
HE'S ON TV!
SLUP LUP LURP
DOG GONE FUNNY
Mara and David DiDonato's English springer spaniel, of Simsbury, Ct., has a strange habit. She would rather eat the cat's food than her own. So they put her food in the cat's bowl and she gobbles it right down!

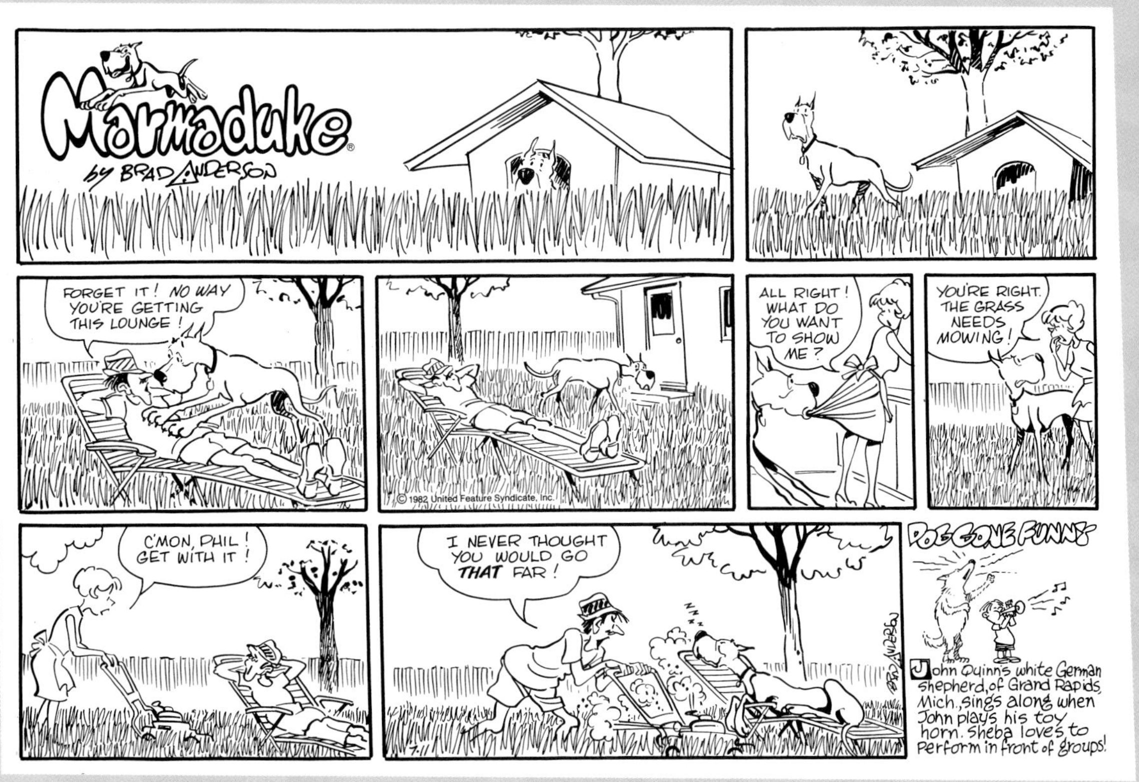
Marmaduke
by Brad Anderson
FORGET IT! NO WAY YOU'RE GETTING THIS LOUNGE!
© 1982 United Feature Syndicate, Inc.
ALL RIGHT! WHAT DO YOU WANT TO SHOW ME?
YOU'RE RIGHT. THE GRASS NEEDS MOWING!
C'MON, PHIL! GET WITH IT!
I NEVER THOUGHT YOU WOULD GO THAT FAR!
DOG GONE FUNNY
John Quinn's white German shepherd, of Grand Rapids, Mich., sings along when John plays his toy horn. Sheba loves to perform in front of groups!

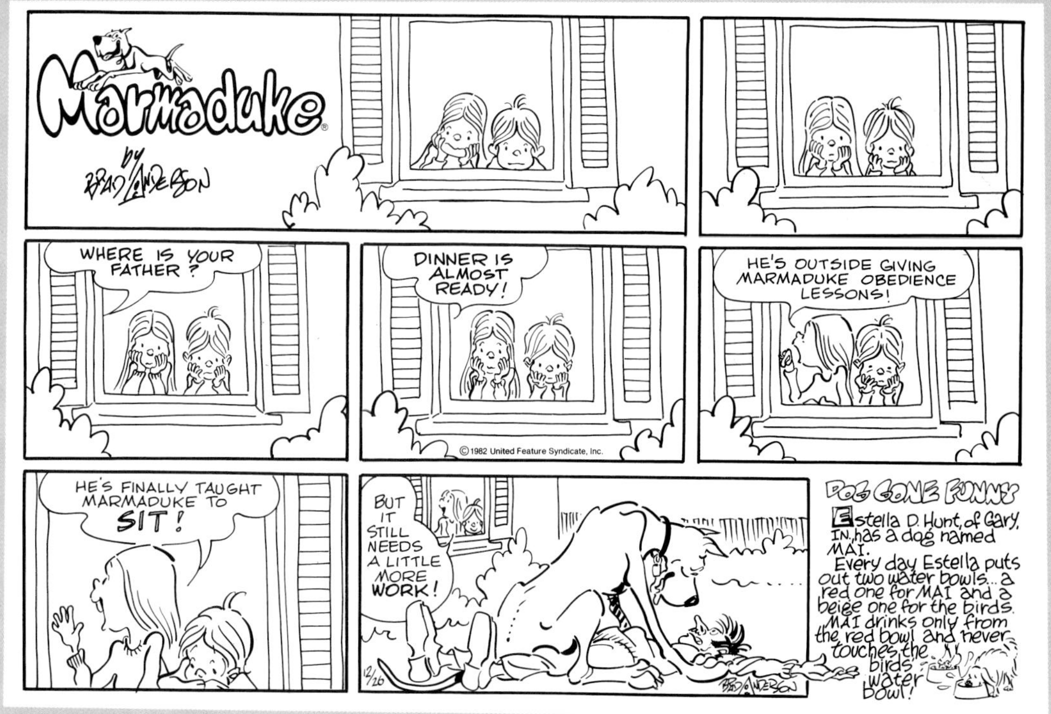
Marmaduke
by Brad Anderson
WHERE IS YOUR FATHER?
DINNER IS ALMOST READY!
HE'S OUTSIDE GIVING MARMADUKE OBEDIENCE LESSONS!
© 1982 United Feature Syndicate, Inc.
HE'S FINALLY TAUGHT MARMADUKE TO SIT!
BUT IT STILL NEEDS A LITTLE MORE WORK!
DOG GONE FUNNY
Estella D. Hunt, of Gary, IN, has a dog named MAI.
Every day Estella puts out two water bowls... a red one for MAI and a beige one for the birds. MAI drinks only from the red bowl and never touches the birds' water bowl!

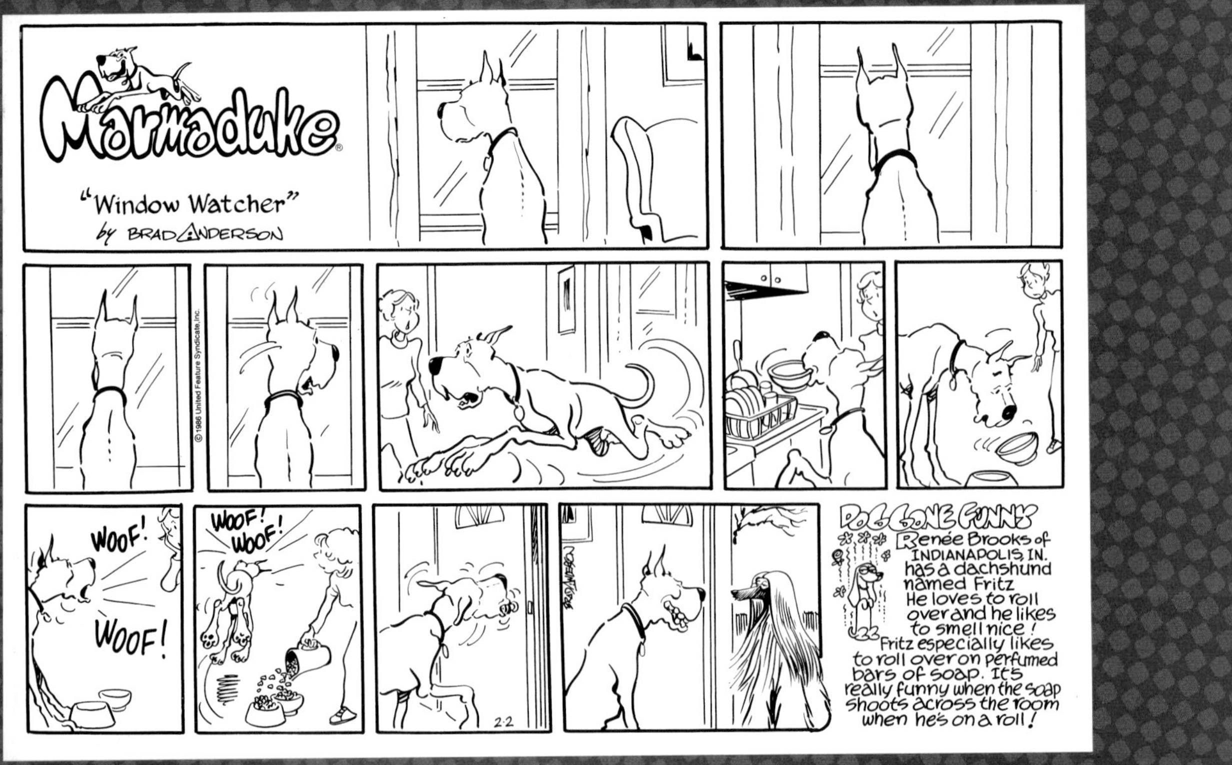
Marmaduke
"Window Watcher"
by BRAD ANDERSON
© 1986 United Feature Syndicate, Inc.
WOOF!
WOOF!
WOOF!
WOOF!
2-2
DOGGONE FUNNY
Renée Brooks of INDIANAPOLIS, IN. has a dachshund named Fritz. He loves to roll over and he likes to smell nice! Fritz especially likes to roll over on perfumed bars of soap. It's really funny when the soap shoots across the room when he's on a roll!

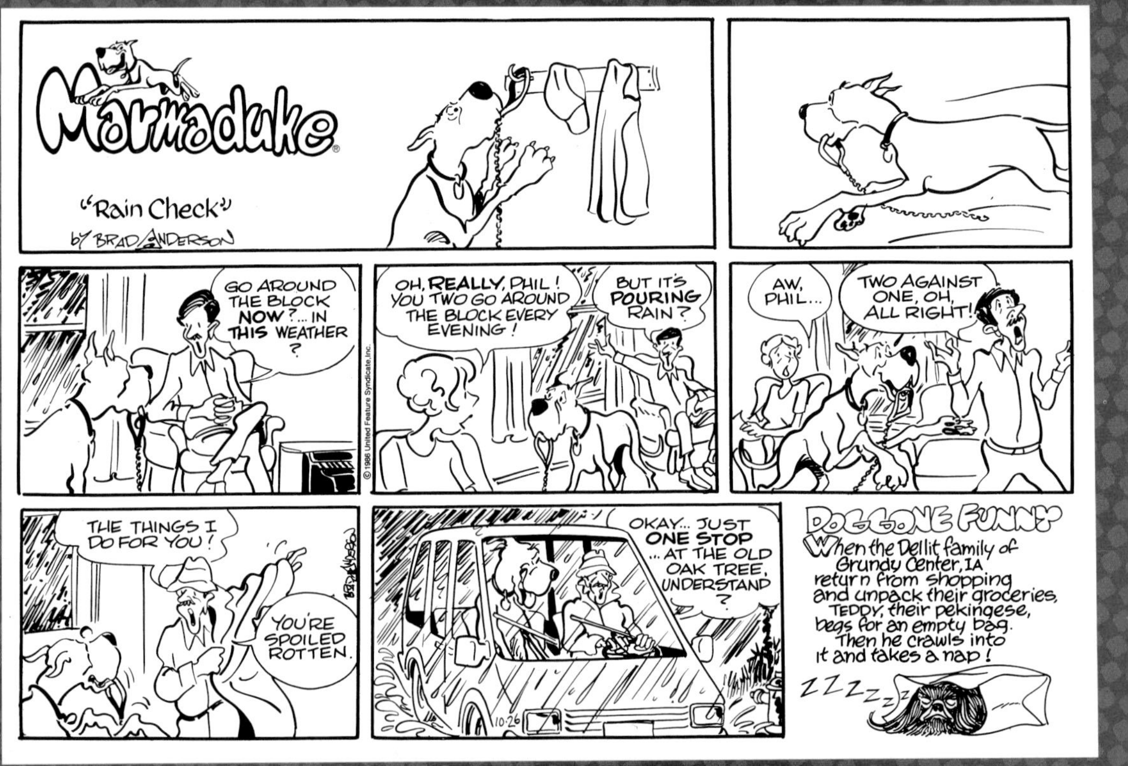
Marmaduke
"Rain Check"
by BRAD ANDERSON
GO AROUND THE BLOCK NOW?... IN THIS WEATHER?
© 1986 United Feature Syndicate, Inc.
OH, REALLY, PHIL! YOU TWO GO AROUND THE BLOCK EVERY EVENING!
BUT IT'S POURING RAIN?
AW, PHIL...
TWO AGAINST ONE, OH, ALL RIGHT!
THE THINGS I DO FOR YOU!
YOU'RE SPOILED ROTTEN.
OKAY... JUST ONE STOP ... AT THE OLD OAK TREE, UNDERSTAND?
10-26
DOGGONE FUNNY
When the Dellit family of Grundy Center, IA return from shopping and unpack their groceries, TEDDY, their pekingese, begs for an empty bag. Then he crawls into it and takes a nap!
ZZZZZZ

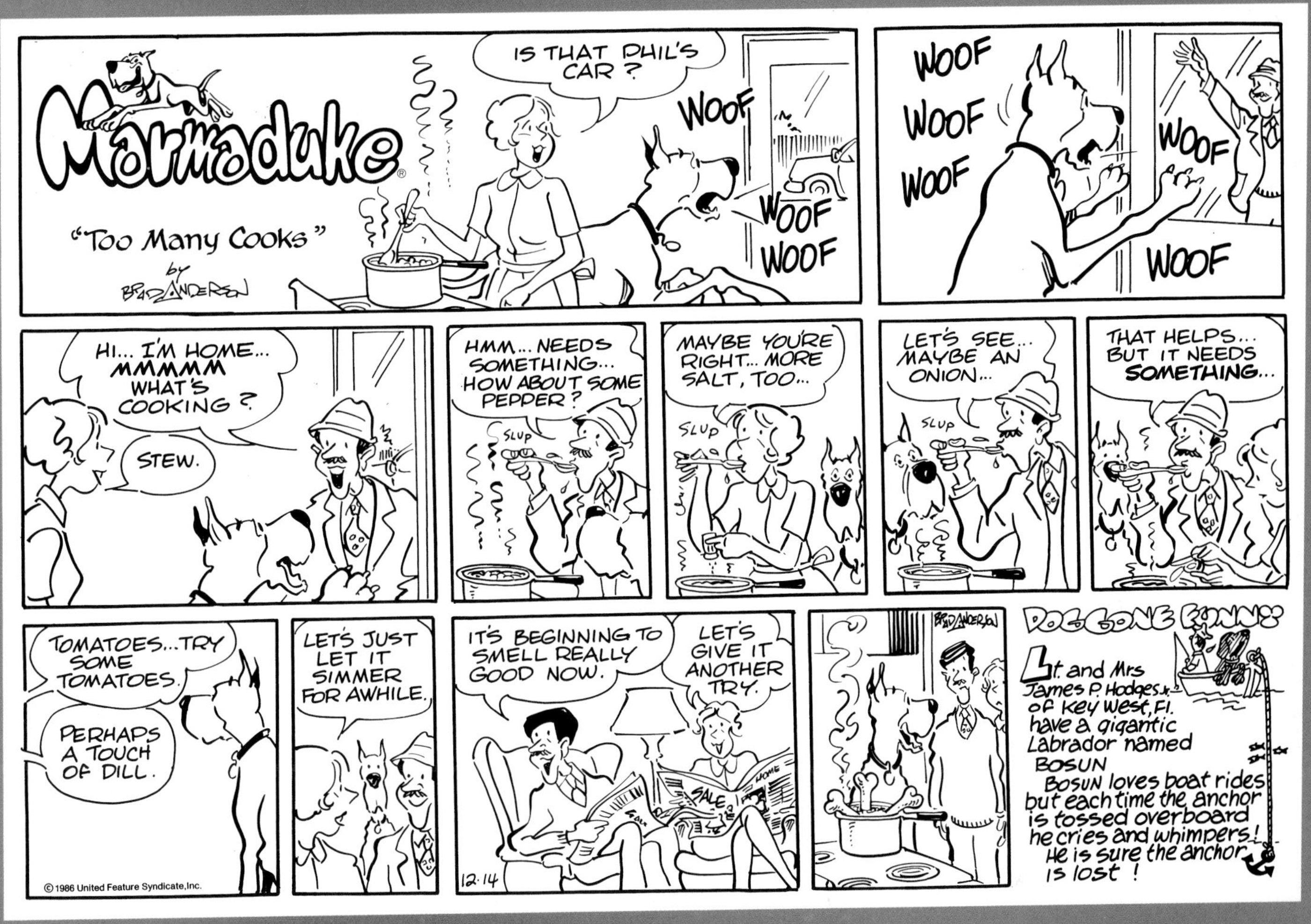
Marmaduke
"Too Many Cooks"
by BRAD ANDERSON
IS THAT PHIL'S CAR ?
WOOF
WOOF
WOOF
WOOF
WOOF
WOOF
WOOF
WOOF
HI... I'M HOME... MMMMM WHAT'S COOKING ?
STEW.
HMM... NEEDS SOMETHING... HOW ABOUT SOME PEPPER ?
SLUP
MAYBE YOU'RE RIGHT... MORE SALT, TOO...
SLUP
LET'S SEE... MAYBE AN ONION...
SLUP
THAT HELPS... BUT IT NEEDS SOMETHING...
TOMATOES...TRY SOME TOMATOES.
PERHAPS A TOUCH OF DILL.
© 1986 United Feature Syndicate, Inc.
LET'S JUST LET IT SIMMER FOR AWHILE.
IT'S BEGINNING TO SMELL REALLY GOOD NOW.
LET'S GIVE IT ANOTHER TRY.
SALE
HOME
12·14
BRAD ANDERSON
DOGGONE FUNNY
Lt. and Mrs James P. Hodges Jr. of Key West, Fl. have a gigantic Labrador named BOSUN
BOSUN loves boat rides but each time the anchor is tossed overboard he cries and whimpers! He is sure the anchor is lost !

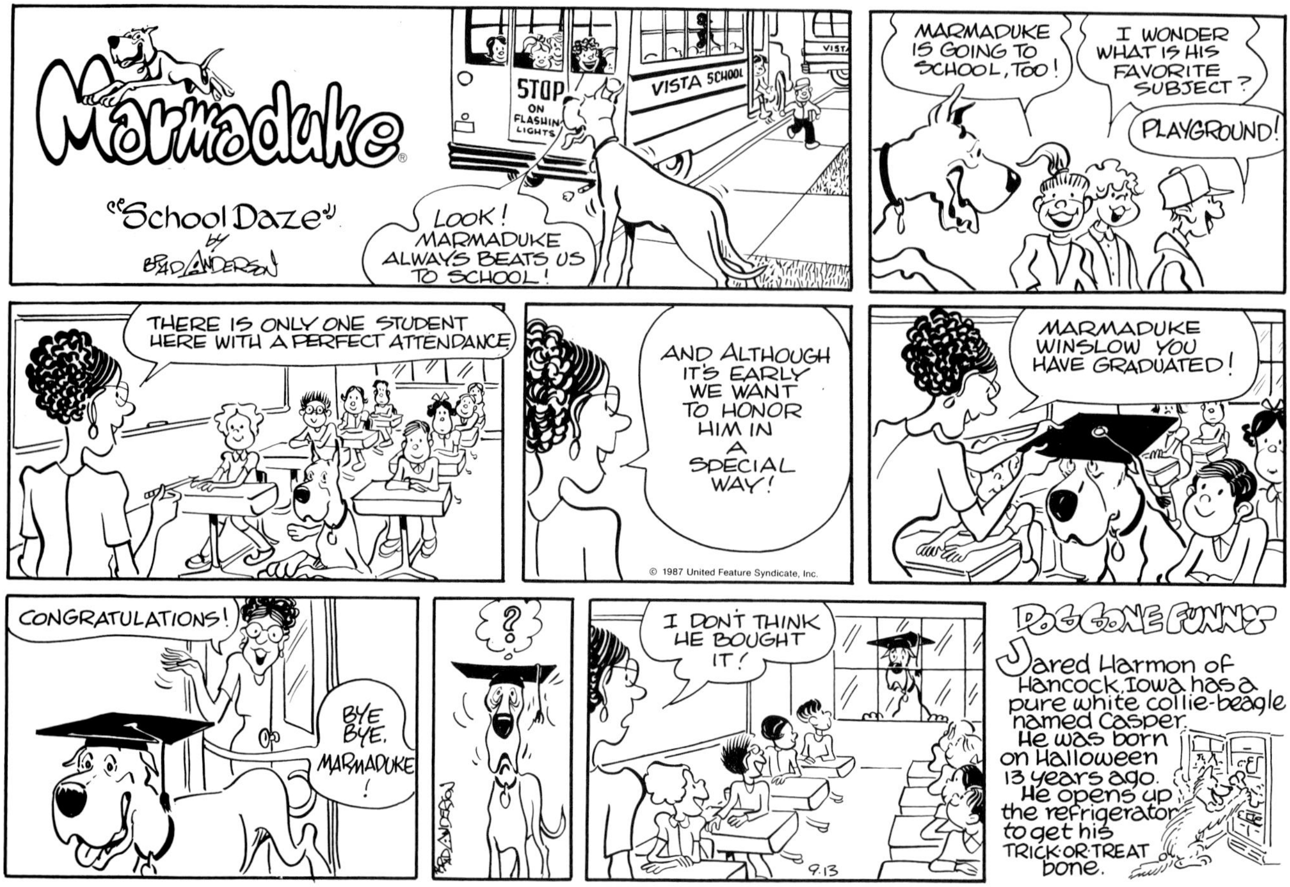
Marmaduke
"School Daze"
by Brad Anderson
STOP ON FLASHING LIGHTS
VISTA SCHOOL
LOOK! MARMADUKE ALWAYS BEATS US TO SCHOOL!
MARMADUKE IS GOING TO SCHOOL, TOO!
I WONDER WHAT IS HIS FAVORITE SUBJECT?
PLAYGROUND!
THERE IS ONLY ONE STUDENT HERE WITH A PERFECT ATTENDANCE
AND ALTHOUGH IT'S EARLY WE WANT TO HONOR HIM IN A SPECIAL WAY!
© 1987 United Feature Syndicate, Inc.
MARMADUKE WINSLOW YOU HAVE GRADUATED!
CONGRATULATIONS!
BYE BYE, MARMADUKE!
?
I DON'T THINK HE BOUGHT IT!
9-13
DOGGONE FUNNY
Jared Harmon of Hancock, Iowa has a pure white collie-beagle named Casper. He was born on Halloween 13 years ago. He opens up the refrigerator to get his TRICK-OR-TREAT bone.

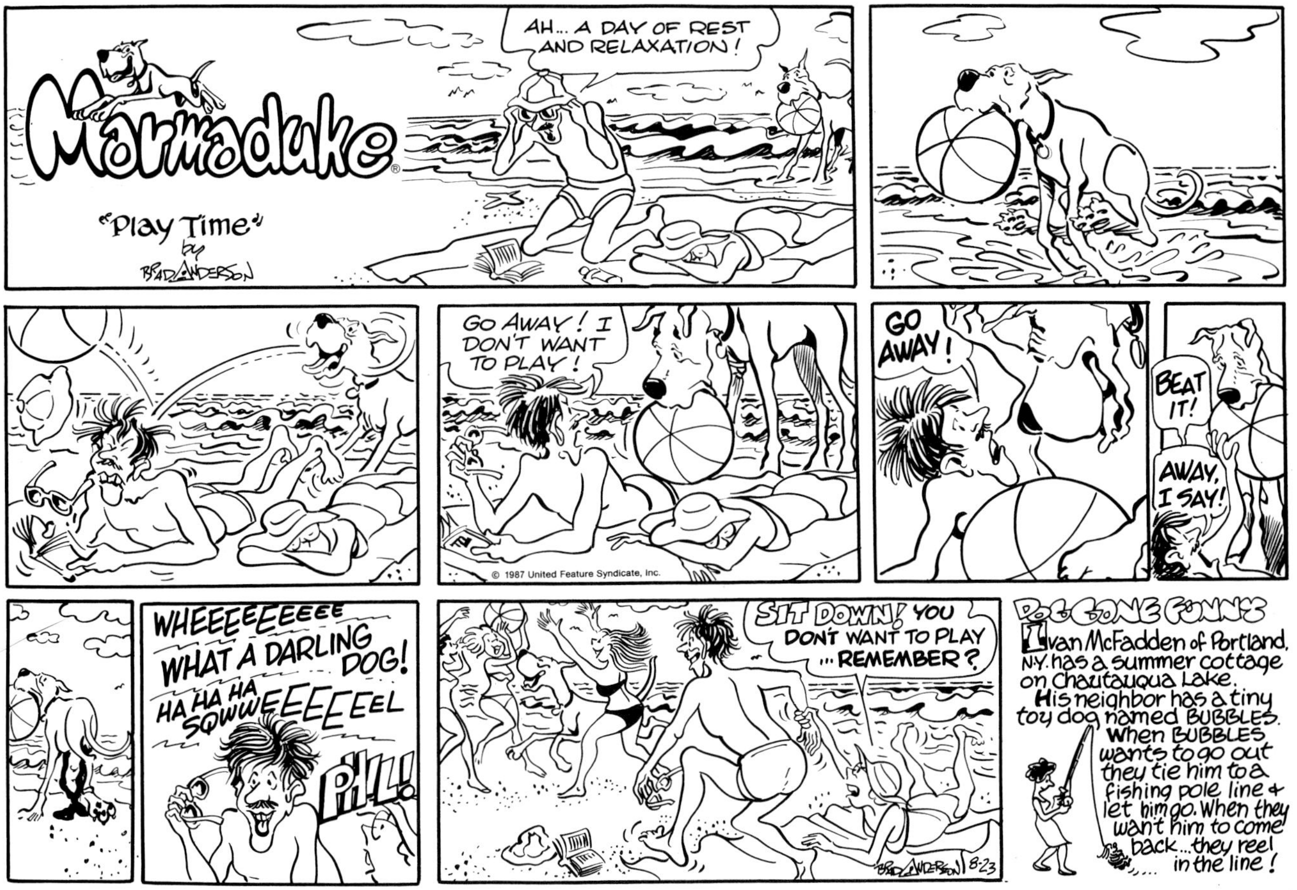
Marmaduke
"Play Time"
by
Brad Anderson
AH... A DAY OF REST AND RELAXATION!
GO AWAY! I DON'T WANT TO PLAY!
© 1987 United Feature Syndicate, Inc.
GO AWAY!
BEAT IT!
AWAY, I SAY!
WHEEEEEEEEEE
WHAT A DARLING DOG!
HA HA HA
SQWWEEEEEEEL
PHIL!
SIT DOWN! YOU DON'T WANT TO PLAY ... REMEMBER?
Brad Anderson 8-23
DOG GONE FUNNY
Ivan McFadden of Portland, N.Y. has a summer cottage on Chautauqua Lake.
His neighbor has a tiny toy dog named BUBBLES.
When BUBBLES wants to go out they tie him to a fishing pole line & let him go. When they want him to come back... they reel in the line!

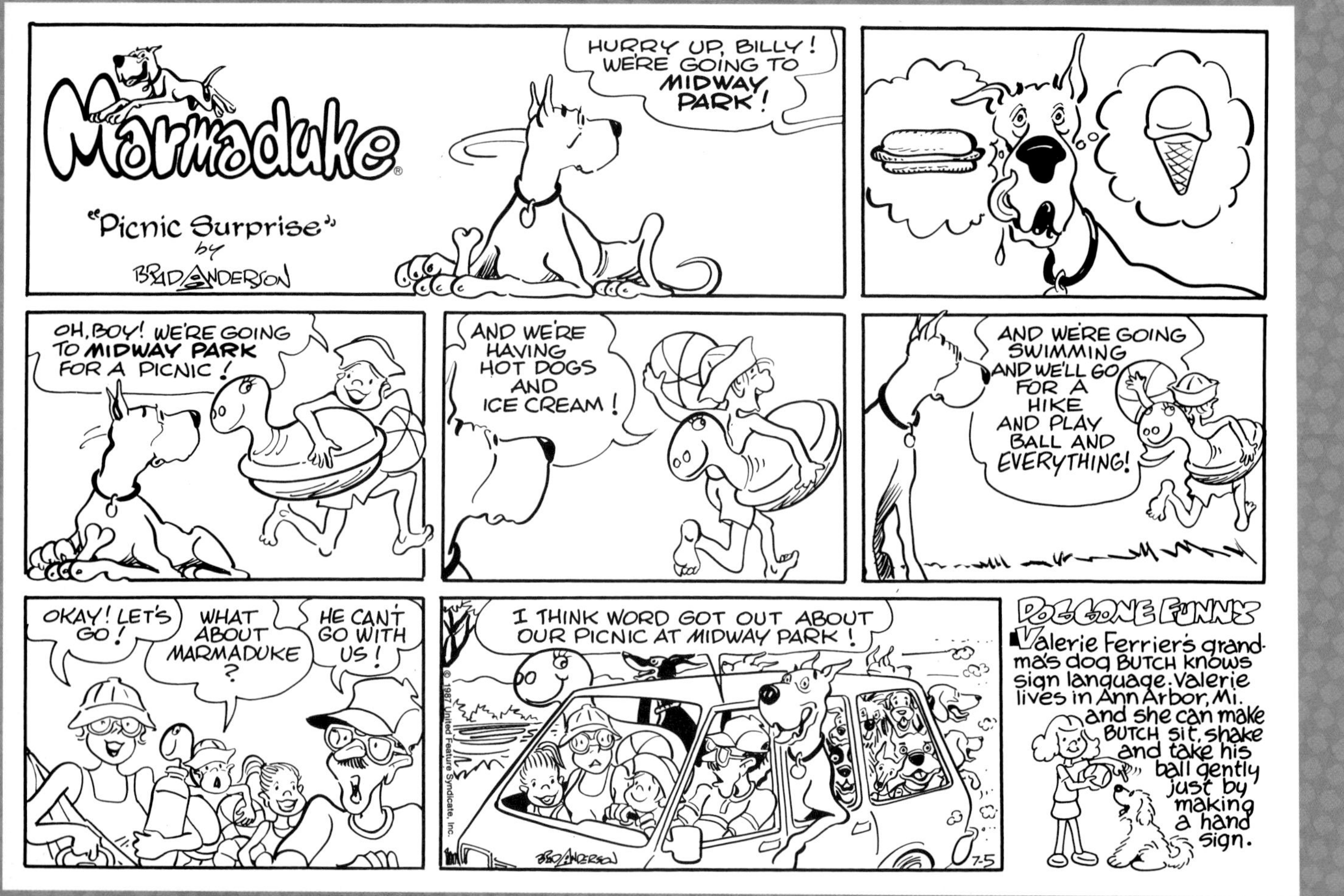
Marmaduke
"Picnic Surprise"
by
BRAD ANDERSON
HURRY UP, BILLY! WE'RE GOING TO MIDWAY PARK!
OH, BOY! WE'RE GOING TO MIDWAY PARK FOR A PICNIC!
AND WE'RE HAVING HOT DOGS AND ICE CREAM!
AND WE'RE GOING SWIMMING AND WE'LL GO FOR A HIKE AND PLAY BALL AND EVERYTHING!
OKAY! LET'S GO!
WHAT ABOUT MARMADUKE?
HE CAN'T GO WITH US!
I THINK WORD GOT OUT ABOUT OUR PICNIC AT MIDWAY PARK!
© 1987 United Feature Syndicate, Inc.
BRAD ANDERSON
7-5
DOGGONE FUNNY
Valerie Ferrier's grandma's dog BUTCH knows sign language. Valerie lives in Ann Arbor, Mi. and she can make BUTCH sit, shake and take his ball gently just by making a hand sign.

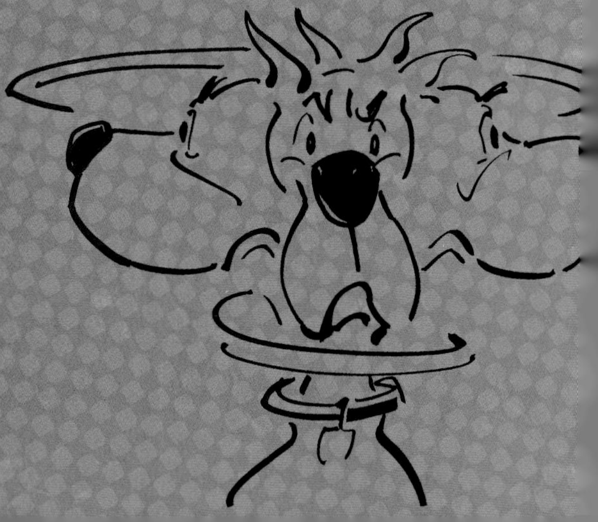

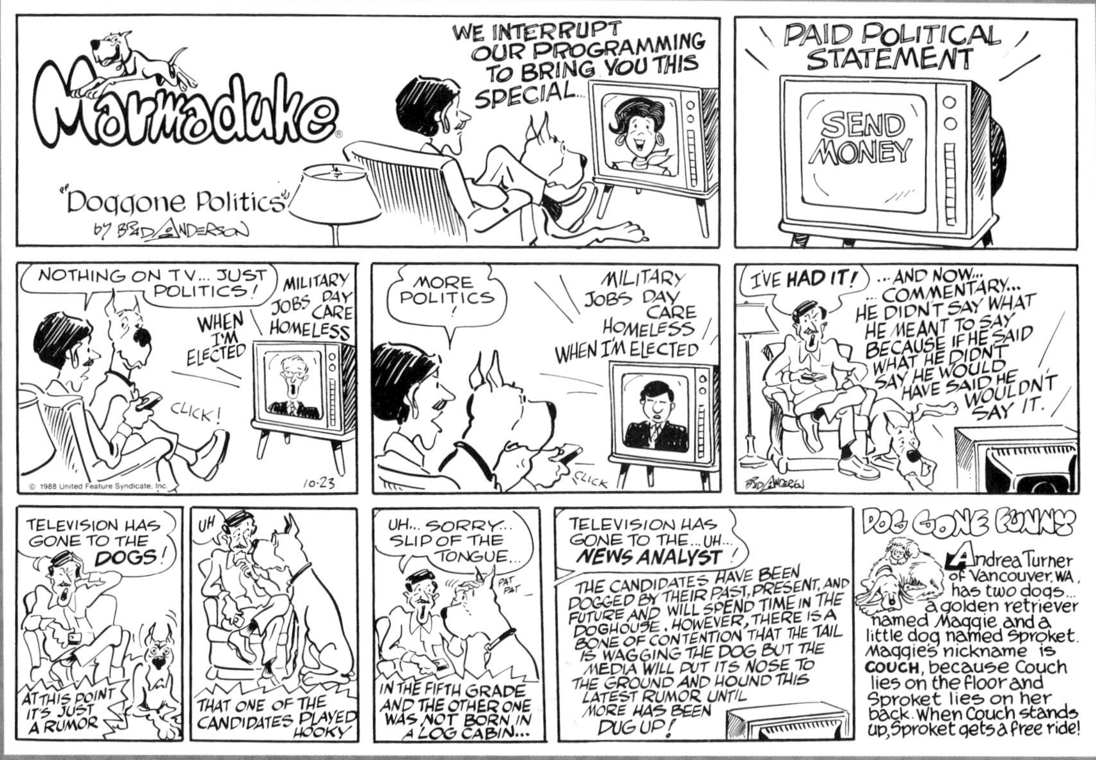

Marmaduke
"Doggone Politics"
by Brad Anderson
WE INTERRUPT OUR PROGRAMMING TO BRING YOU THIS SPECIAL...
PAID POLITICAL STATEMENT
SEND MONEY
NOTHING ON TV... JUST POLITICS!
MILITARY JOBS DAY CARE HOMELESS
WHEN I'M ELECTED
CLICK!
© 1988 United Feature Syndicate, Inc.
10-23
MORE POLITICS!
MILITARY JOBS DAY CARE HOMELESS WHEN I'M ELECTED
CLICK
I'VE HAD IT!
...AND NOW... ...COMMENTARY... HE DIDN'T SAY WHAT HE MEANT TO SAY BECAUSE IF HE SAID WHAT HE DIDN'T SAY HE WOULD HAVE SAID HE WOULDN'T SAY IT.
TELEVISION HAS GONE TO THE DOGS!
AT THIS POINT IT'S JUST A RUMOR
UH
THAT ONE OF THE CANDIDATES PLAYED HOOKY
UH... SORRY... SLIP OF THE TONGUE...
PAT PAT
IN THE FIFTH GRADE AND THE OTHER ONE WAS NOT BORN IN A LOG CABIN...
TELEVISION HAS GONE TO THE... UH... NEWS ANALYST!
THE CANDIDATES HAVE BEEN DOGGED BY THEIR PAST, PRESENT, AND FUTURE AND WILL SPEND TIME IN THE DOGHOUSE. HOWEVER, THERE IS A BONE OF CONTENTION THAT THE TAIL IS WAGGING THE DOG BUT THE MEDIA WILL PUT ITS NOSE TO THE GROUND AND HOUND THIS LATEST RUMOR UNTIL MORE HAS BEEN DUG UP!
DOG GONE FUNNY
Andrea Turner of Vancouver, WA, has two dogs... a golden retriever named Maggie and a little dog named Sproket. Maggie's nickname is COUCH, because Couch lies on the floor and Sproket lies on her back. When Couch stands up, Sproket gets a free ride!

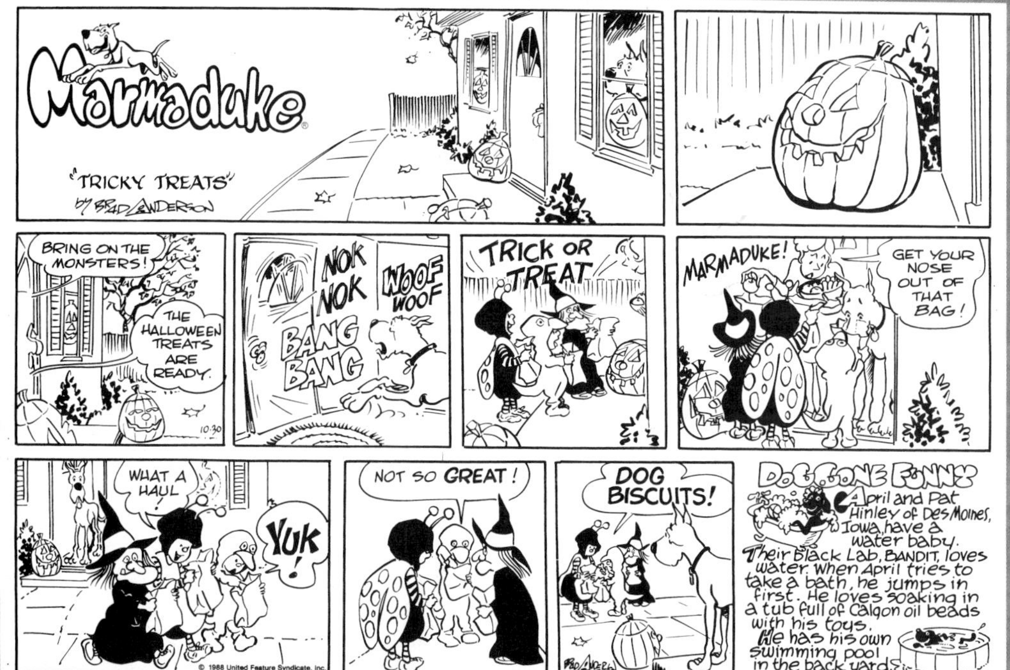

Marmaduke
"TRICKY TREATS"
by Brad Anderson
BRING ON THE MONSTERS!
THE HALLOWEEN TREATS ARE READY.
10-30
NOK NOK
WOOF WOOF
BANG BANG
TRICK OR TREAT
MARMADUKE!
GET YOUR NOSE OUT OF THAT BAG!
WHAT A HAUL
YUK!
© 1988 United Feature Syndicate, Inc.
NOT SO GREAT!
DOG BISCUITS!
DOG GONE FUNNY
April and Pat Hinley of Des Moines, Iowa, have a water baby. Their Black Lab, BANDIT, loves water. When April tries to take a bath, he jumps in first. He loves soaking in a tub full of Calgon oil beads with his toys. He has his own swimming pool in the back yard.

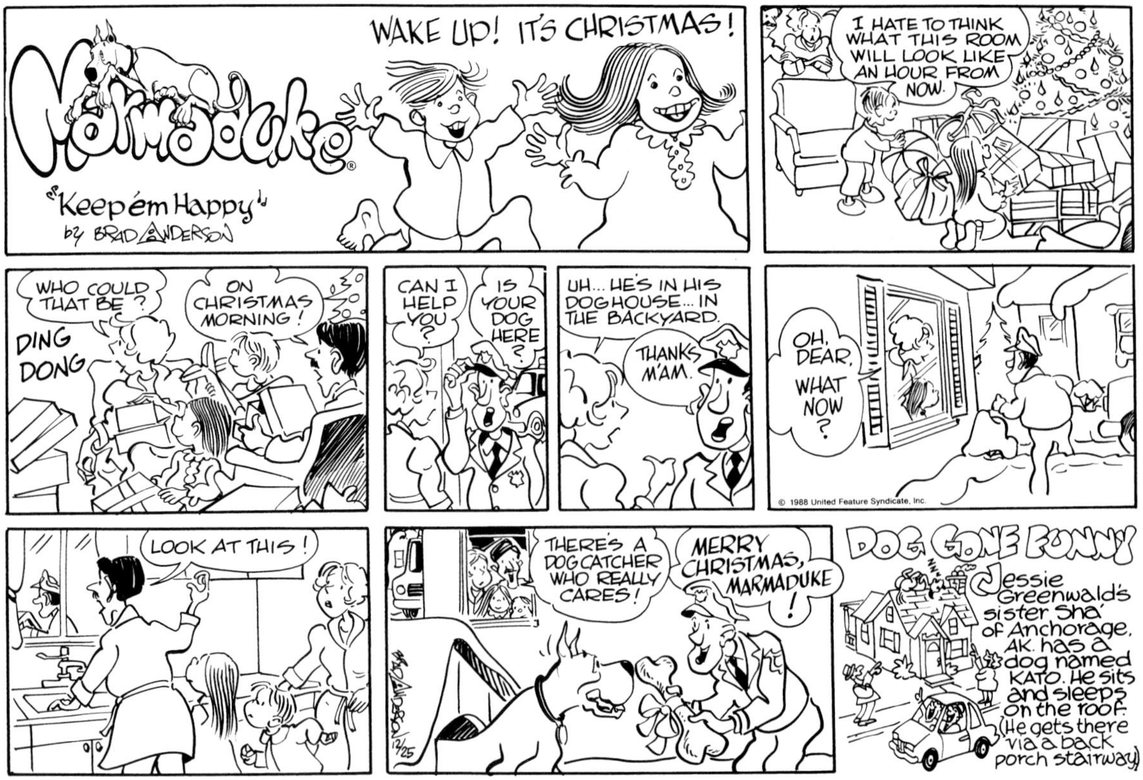
Marmaduke
"Keep'em Happy"
by BRAD ANDERSON
WAKE UP! IT'S CHRISTMAS!
I HATE TO THINK WHAT THIS ROOM WILL LOOK LIKE AN HOUR FROM NOW.
WHO COULD THAT BE?
DING DONG
ON CHRISTMAS MORNING!
CAN I HELP YOU?
IS YOUR DOG HERE?
UH... HE'S IN HIS DOGHOUSE... IN THE BACKYARD.
THANKS M'AM.
OH, DEAR, WHAT NOW?
© 1988 United Feature Syndicate, Inc.
LOOK AT THIS!
THERE'S A DOGCATCHER WHO REALLY CARES!
MERRY CHRISTMAS, MARMADUKE!
12/25
DOG GONE FUNNY
Jessie Greenwald's sister Sha' of Anchorage, AK. has a dog named KATO. He sits and sleeps on the roof. (He gets there via a back porch stairway)

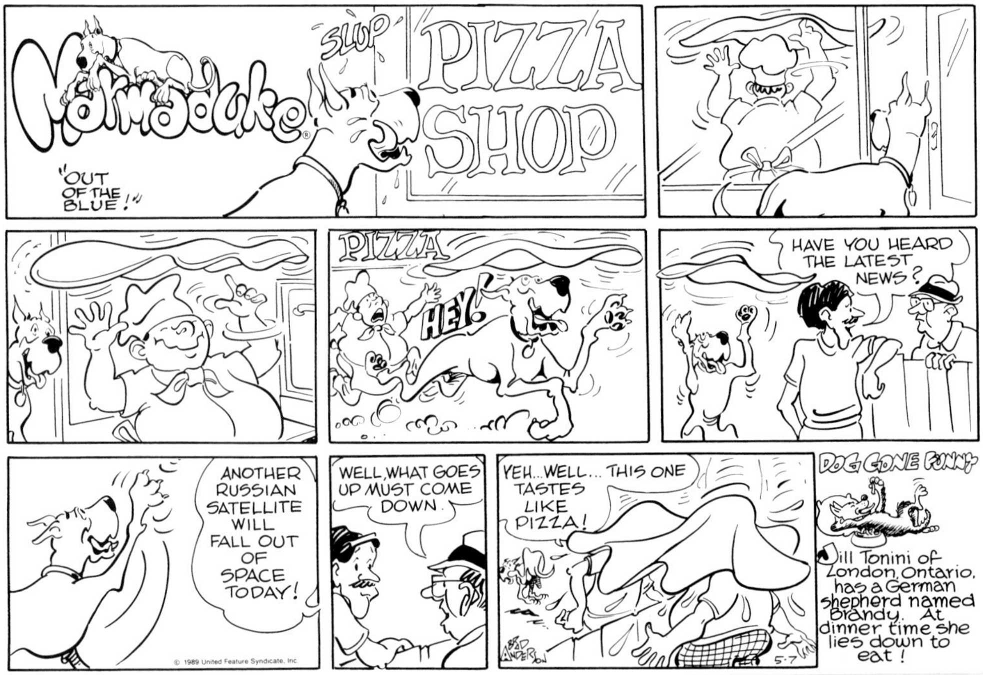
Marmaduke
"OUT OF THE BLUE!"
SLOP
PIZZA SHOP
PIZZA
HEY!
HAVE YOU HEARD THE LATEST NEWS?
ANOTHER RUSSIAN SATELLITE WILL FALL OUT OF SPACE TODAY!
© 1989 United Feature Syndicate, Inc.
WELL, WHAT GOES UP MUST COME DOWN.
YEH...WELL... THIS ONE TASTES LIKE PIZZA!
5-7
DOG GONE FUNNY
Jill Tonini of London, Ontario, has a German shepherd named Brandy. At dinner time she lies down to eat!

Marmaduke
"In Training"
PARKS and RECREATION
DOG OBEDIENCE CLASS TODAY 3:00 P.M.
OBEDIEN CLASS TODAY
HURRY, MAC... YOU'VE GOT TO SEE THIS!
PARKS and RECREATION DOG OBEDIENCE CLASS TODAY 3:00 PM
8-6
WHAT'S HAPPENING?
IT'S MARMADUKE. YOU WON'T BELIEVE THIS!
© 1989 United Feature Syndicate, Inc.
HAVE YOU EVER SEEN ANYTHING LIKE THIS?
IT'S HARD TO BELIEVE.
GOOD BOY!
BRAVO!
THAT'S IT, FOLKS... SHOW'S OVER!
GOOD SHOW!
REMARKABLE, MARMADUKE!
GOOD WORK!
CLAP
CLAP
CLAP
CLAP
STOP LOOKING SO SMUG, MARMADUKE!
THEY JUST WENT ALONG WITH THE JOKE...
THEY DON'T REALLY THINK I'M YOUR PET!
DOG GONE FUNNY
SO I SAID TO HER...
YAWN
Eileen Panek of San Marcos, CA, and her senior-citizen companions have a poodle, Tina. They talk to Tina as if she were human. When Tina tires of the conversation, she takes her baby blanket in her mouth, puts it on a lap, and NAPS.

"ZZZZZZ"
Marmaduke
OOF
VETERINARIAN
DOCTOR, HERE COMES MARMADUKE!
OH, BOY! I HOPE MY INSURANCE POLICY IS PAID UP!
PUT HIM UP HERE
© 1989 United Feature Syndicate, Inc.
I'M REALLY WORRIED
UMM
HMMM
HAS HE LOST HIS WILL TO LIVE?
UMMM
WELL... NOT EXACTLY.
WHAT'S HIS PROBLEM, PHIL?
AN INCURABLE CASE OF DOG DAYS LAZINESS!
8-27
DOG GONE FUNNY
When Theresa Glashaw of St. Ignace, MI, rides her 4-wheeler, her schnauzer waits to be invited. Theresa says, "Do you want to come?" and Schatzie jumps aboard. When the ride is over, he sits there until told, "Get off!"

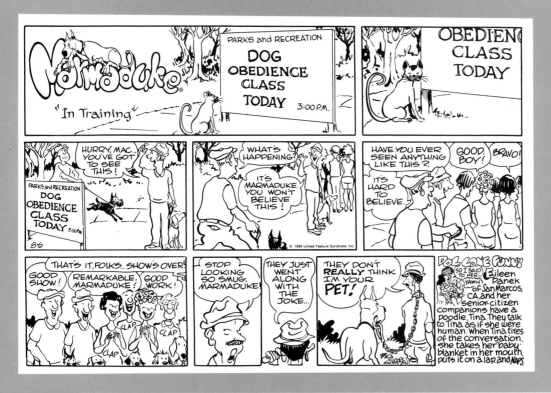

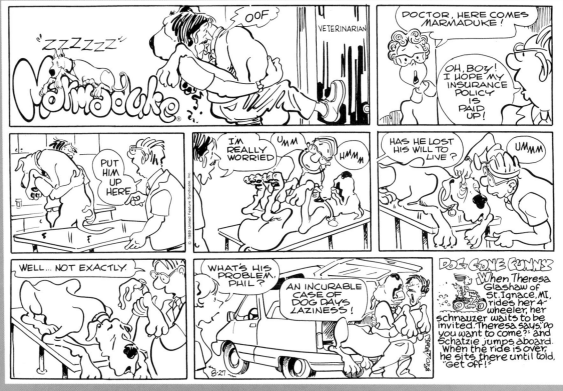

Marmaduke®
Chair Share
Z Z Z Z
MY CHAIR
MY CHAIR!... THIS WILL REQUIRE SOME PSYCHOLOGY TO MAKE HIM MOVE!
© 1989 United Feature Syndicate, Inc.
HERE COMES THE ICE CREAM WAGON!
WHO WANTS SOME ICE CREAM?
10-8
HERE COMES THE PARCEL DELIVERY MAN!
HERE COMES VERONICA
THIS ALWAYS WORKS!
DING! DONG!
MARMADUKE! GET OUT OF THAT CHAIR!
HERE'S YOUR CHAIR, DAD!
SOMETIMES I FORGET... HE'S JUST A DOG.
SALE
DAILY
DOG GONE FUNNY
WUF WUF
Gordon and Vicki Sanders live in South Portsmouth, KY, with their year-old cocker spaniel, Tippy. Tippy likes to sit on the back of the sofa and look out the window. In the evening, she sees her reflection in the window and barks at the strange dog.

Marmaduke®
Pigskin Fan
DID YOU LEAVE THE TV ON, PHIL?
YES, IT SEEMS TO BE COMPANY FOR MARMADUKE.
AND HE LOVES FOOTBALL!
7 SECONDS LEFT TO PLAY AND VERVOVICH PASSES LONG... DEEP...
WUF
11-26
TO SEELY... IN THE END ZONE...
20
...WHO...
WOOF
...IS...
...IN...
...THE CLEAR...
© 1989 United Feature Syndicate, Inc.
BUT SEELY HAS, FROZEN... HE CAN'T MOVE...
WOOF
WOOF
AND THE BALL SEEMS TO HAVE DISAPPEARED...
DOG GONE FUNNY
MMM SLURP MMM
Karen Freeman of Hayward, CA has a terrier named Amanda, with a sweet tooth. Amanda gets into Karen's purse and eats her Tootsie pops. However, she leaves the wrapper and stick.

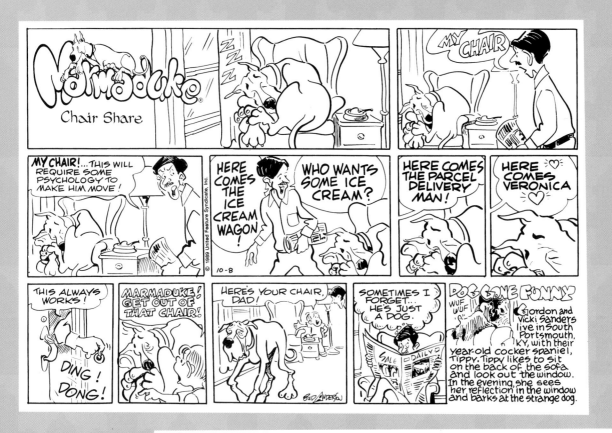

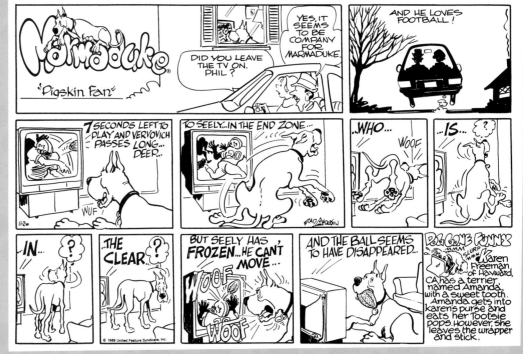

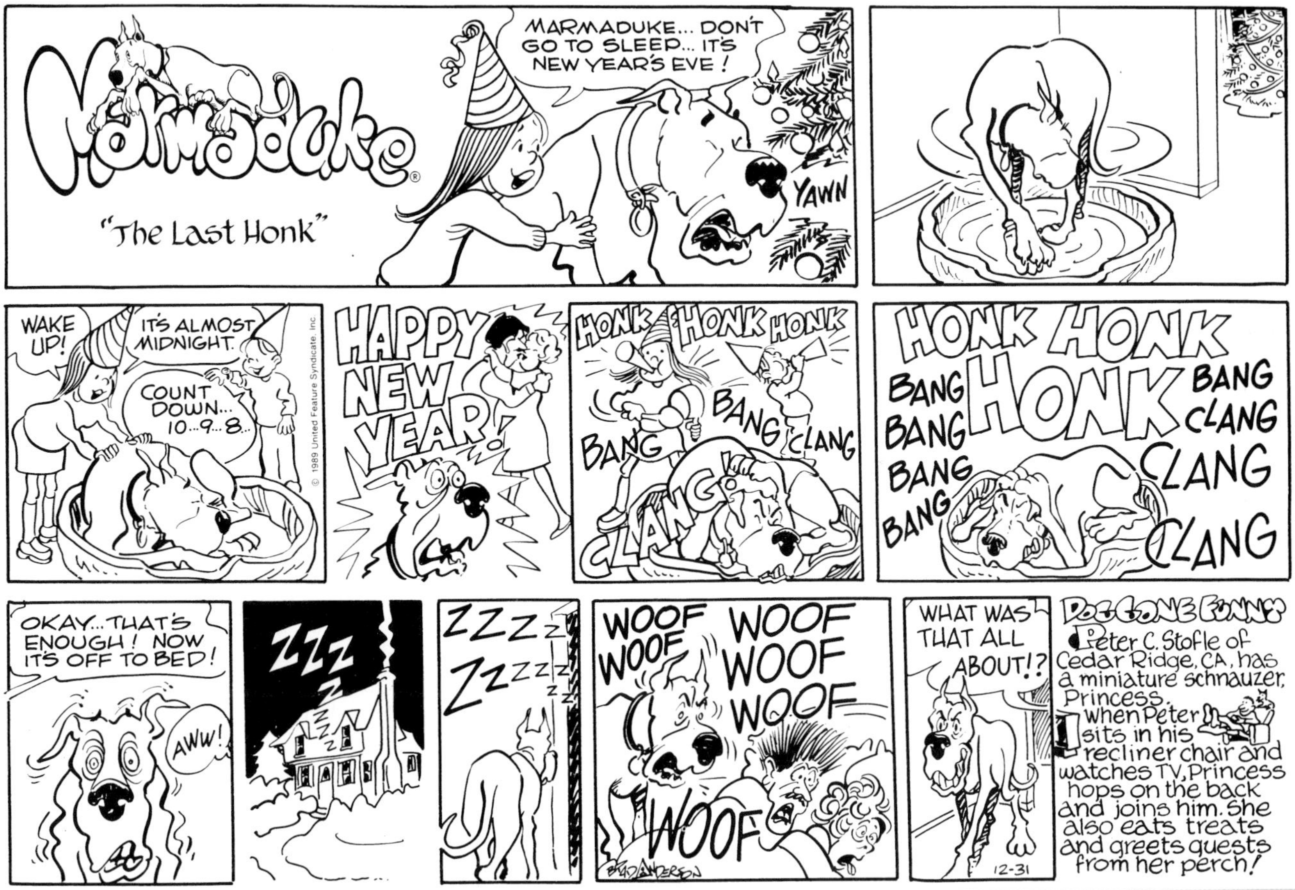

Marmaduke
"The Last Honk"
MARMADUKE... DON'T GO TO SLEEP... IT'S NEW YEAR'S EVE!
YAWN
WAKE UP!
IT'S ALMOST MIDNIGHT.
COUNT DOWN... 10...9...8...
© 1989 United Feature Syndicate, Inc.
HAPPY NEW YEAR!
HONK HONK HONK
BANG BANG CLANG
BANG
CLANG!
HONK HONK
BANG BANG HONK BANG CLANG
BANG BANG
CLANG
CLANG
OKAY... THAT'S ENOUGH! NOW IT'S OFF TO BED!
AWW!
ZZZ
ZZZZZ
ZZZZZ
WOOF WOOF WOOF WOOF WOOF
WOOF
WOOF
BRAD ANDERSON
WHAT WAS THAT ALL ABOUT!?
12-31
DOG GONE FUNNY
Peter C. Stofle of Cedar Ridge, CA, has a miniature schnauzer, Princess. When Peter sits in his recliner chair and watches TV, Princess hops on the back and joins him. She also eats treats and greets guests from her perch!

Marmaduke®
in
"Snow No, No"
1-5-97
© 1996 United Feature Syndicate, Inc.
HEY, YOU... YOU...
UHH...
THAT'S IMPOSSIBLE.
WHOEVER HEARD OF A DOG THROWING A SNOWBALL?
DOG GONE FUNNYS
Bob & Fannie Kutz of Hayward, WI, have a Siberian husky, Peppy, and a cat, Kitzi.
They eat together.
They sleep together.
And sometimes they "nose" each other.

Marmaduke®
in
"Snowman's Best Friend"
1-19
© 1997 United Feature Syndicate, Inc.
WOOF WOOF
WOOF
WOOF
WOOF
PHIL! WHAT ARE YOU DOING?
WOOF WOOF WOOF
GUESS.
DOG GONE FUNNYS
Charles H. Mont of Burbank, CA, has a Shar-Pei, Cuddles. When Clementine, an English bulldog, visits, Charles gives Clementine a biscuit first. Then he gives one to Cuddles. Once he gave Cuddles the first biscuit. When Cuddles noticed that Clementine didn't have a biscuit, she stood in front of Clementine as if to offer her the biscuit. Charles quickly gave Clementine a biscuit.

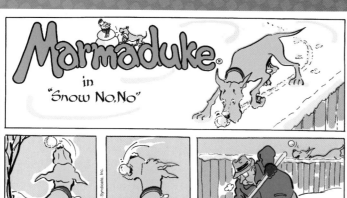

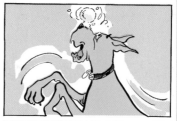

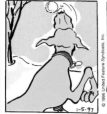

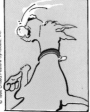

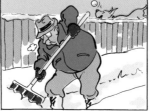

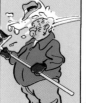

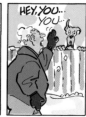

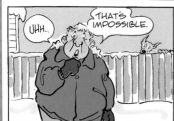

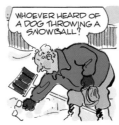

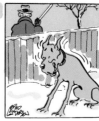

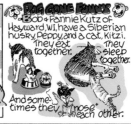

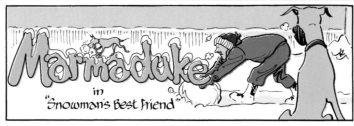

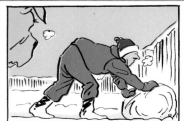

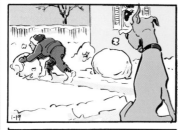

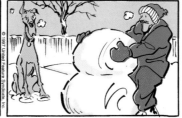

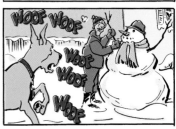

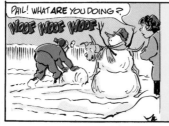

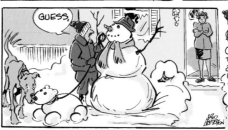

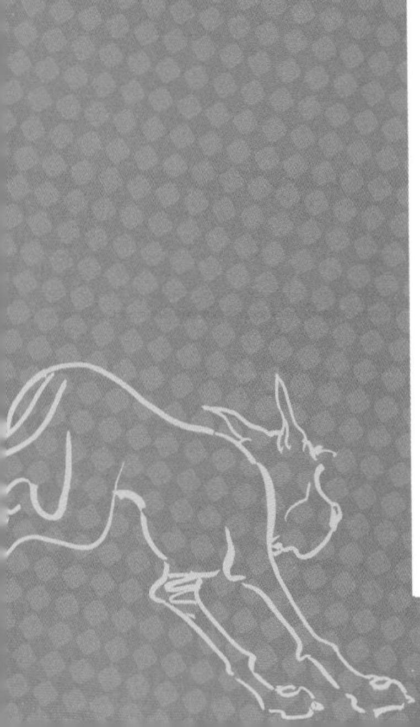

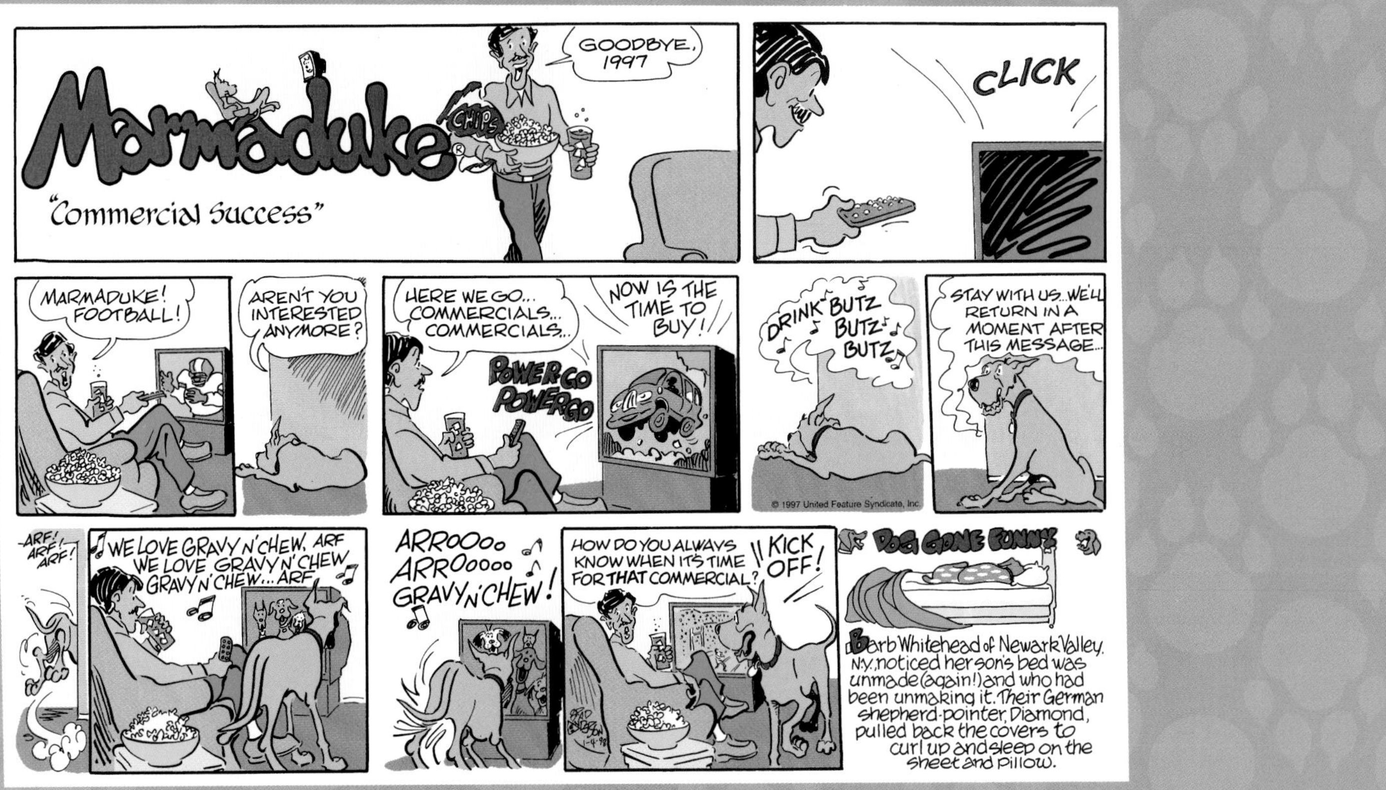
Marmaduke
"Commercial Success"
CHIPS
GOODBYE, 1997
CLICK
MARMADUKE! FOOTBALL!
AREN'T YOU INTERESTED ANYMORE?
HERE WE GO... COMMERCIALS... COMMERCIALS...
NOW IS THE TIME TO BUY!
POWER-GO POWER-GO
DRINK BUTZ BUTZ BUTZ
STAY WITH US...WE'LL RETURN IN A MOMENT AFTER THIS MESSAGE...
© 1997 United Feature Syndicate, Inc.
ARF! ARF! ARF!
WE LOVE GRAVY N'CHEW, ARF WE LOVE GRAVY N'CHEW GRAVY N'CHEW...ARF
ARROOooo ARROOoooo GRAVY N'CHEW!
HOW DO YOU ALWAYS KNOW WHEN IT'S TIME FOR THAT COMMERCIAL?
KICK OFF!
DOG GONE FUNNY!
Barb Whitehead of Newark Valley, N.Y., noticed her son's bed was unmade (again!) and who had been unmaking it. Their German shepherd-pointer, Diamond, pulled back the covers to curl up and sleep on the sheet and pillow.

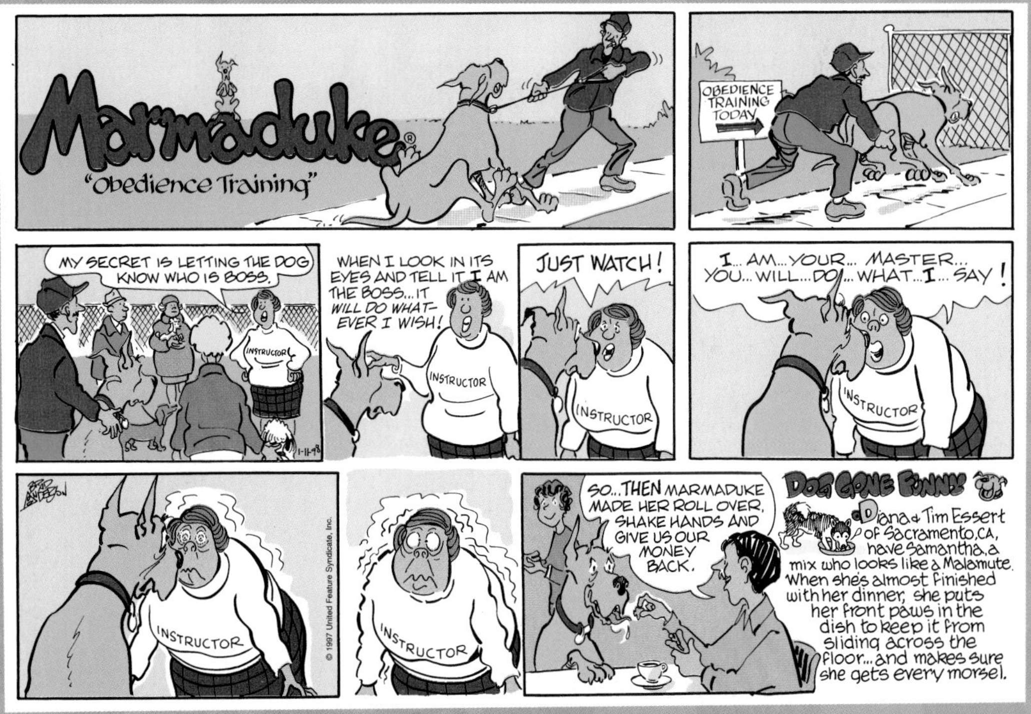
Marmaduke
"Obedience Training"
OBEDIENCE TRAINING TODAY
MY SECRET IS LETTING THE DOG KNOW WHO IS BOSS.
INSTRUCTOR
WHEN I LOOK IN ITS EYES AND TELL IT I AM THE BOSS... IT WILL DO WHATEVER I WISH!
JUST WATCH!
I... AM... YOUR... MASTER... YOU... WILL... DO... WHAT... I... SAY!
© 1997 United Feature Syndicate, Inc.
SO...THEN MARMADUKE MADE HER ROLL OVER, SHAKE HANDS AND GIVE US OUR MONEY BACK.
DOG GONE FUNNY!
Diana & Tim Essert of Sacramento, CA, have Samantha, a mix who looks like a Malamute. When she's almost finished with her dinner, she puts her front paws in the dish to keep it from sliding across the floor...and makes sure she gets every morsel.

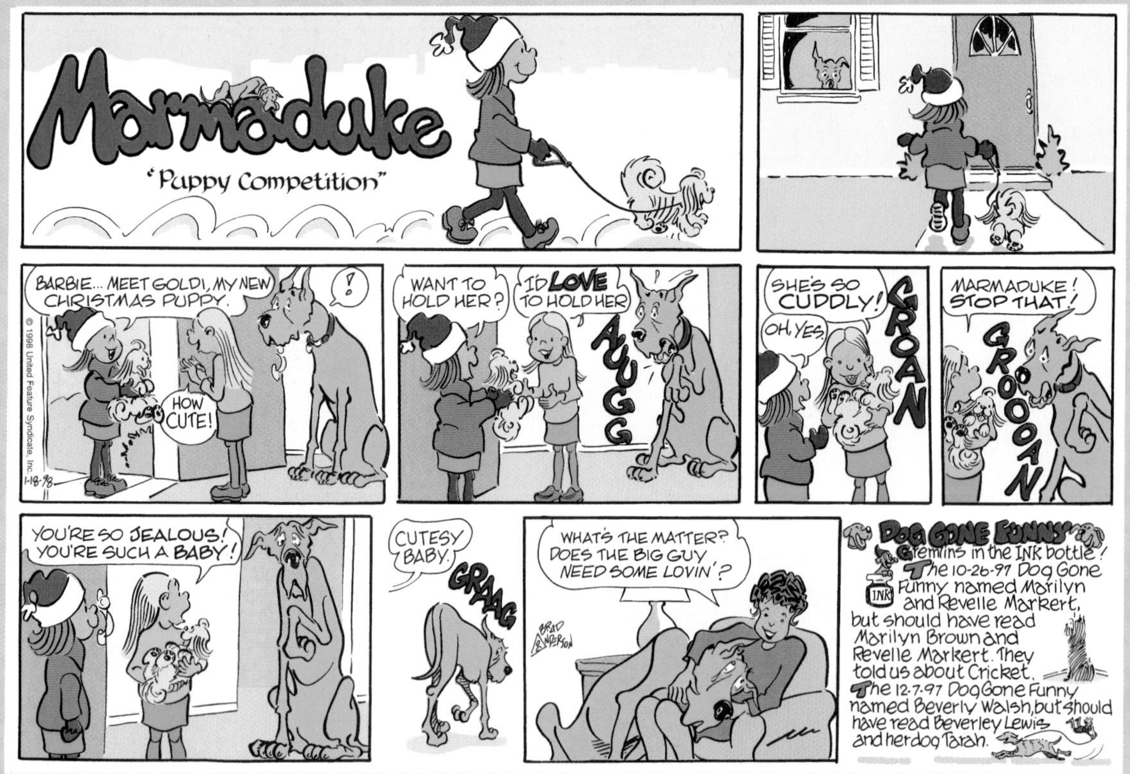
Marmaduke
"Puppy Competition"
BARBIE... MEET GOLDI, MY NEW CHRISTMAS PUPPY.
!
HOW CUTE!
© 1998 United Feature Syndicate, Inc.
1-18-98
WANT TO HOLD HER?
I'D LOVE TO HOLD HER.
AUUGG
SHE'S SO CUDDLY!
OH, YES.
GROAN
MARMADUKE! STOP THAT!
GROOOOAN
YOU'RE SO JEALOUS! YOU'RE SUCH A BABY!
CUTESY BABY.
GRAAAG
WHAT'S THE MATTER? DOES THE BIG GUY NEED SOME LOVIN'?
BRAD ANDERSON
DOG GONE FUNNY
Gremlins in the INK bottle!
The 10-26-97 Dog Gone Funny named Marilyn and Revelle Markert, but should have read Marilyn Brown and Revelle Markert. They told us about Cricket.
The 12-7-97 Dog Gone Funny named Beverly Walsh, but should have read Beverley Lewis and her dog Tarah.

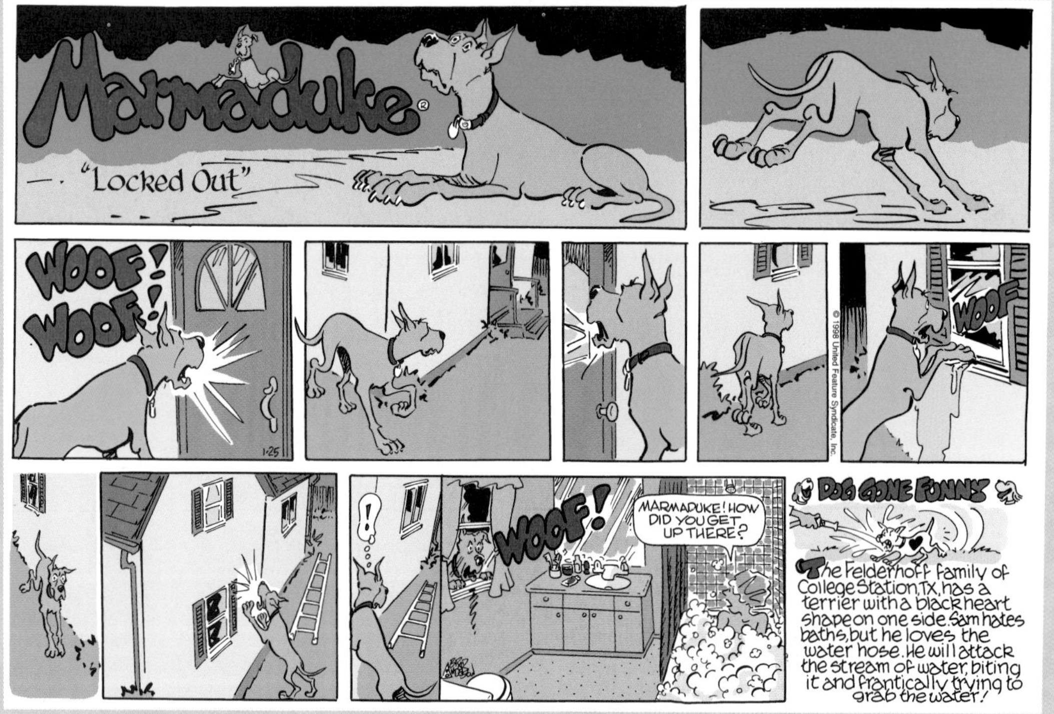
Marmaduke
"Locked Out"
WOOF! WOOF!
1-25
© 1998 United Feature Syndicate, Inc.
WOOF
!
WOOF!
MARMADUKE! HOW DID YOU GET UP THERE?
DOG GONE FUNNY
The Felderhoff family of College Station, TX, has a terrier with a black heart shape on one side. Sam hates baths, but he loves the water hose. He will attack the stream of water, biting it and frantically trying to grab the water!

Marmaduke

"Food for Thought"

LOOK AT THIS WEATHER

DO YOU WANT TO GO FOR YOUR WALK?

GRRRRUMMM

I TAKE IT THAT MEANS NO!

A GOOD DAY TO WATCH SOME MOVIES.

AND MAKE POPCORN.

I HOPE THESE ARE FAMILY MOVIES.

YEAH! SPACE ALIEN FAMILIES.

I RENTED FUNNY MOVIES.

I'LL TRADE YOU SOME CHIPS FOR YOUR POPCORN, DADDY.

OKAY.

CHOMP SLURP

SNIFF SNIFF SNIFF

CHOMF LICK SMUSH

SMAK CHOMF CRUNCH

MARMADUKE! OH, UGH!

WHERE DID HE GET THIS IDEA HE CAN BRING FOOD INTO THE LIVING ROOM?

CHIP-O

DOG GONE FUNNY

Dotty Dixon of Port Richey, FL, wrote and said that their over-12-year-old Rosie sits on her chair at the dinner table. She wears a bib, which has "TODAY I AM A LI'L ANGEL" on one side and "TODAY I AM A LI'L DEVIL" on the other side. Most times Rosie is an angel.

Marmaduke

"TV INTERFERENCE"

THIS SHOW IS SO BORING, I'M GOING TO BED.

MARMADUKE!

GO AWAY!

MARMADUKE! YOU'RE IN MY WAY!

I CAN'T SEE!

BOOM!

I MISSED THE END OF THE MOVIE!

NOW IT'S TIME FOR THE NEWS! DOWN!

GET OFF MY LAP!

OKAY...YOU WIN!

NOW ARE YOU SATISFIED?

SIGH

DOG GONE FUNNY

Jean Foam of Montreal has friends who have an 8-year-old basset hound. Recently they acquired a kitten. Sometimes the kitten rides on the dog's back. When the kitten tires, it falls down and the dog slobbers over it. At bedtime the kitten sleeps on top of the dog.

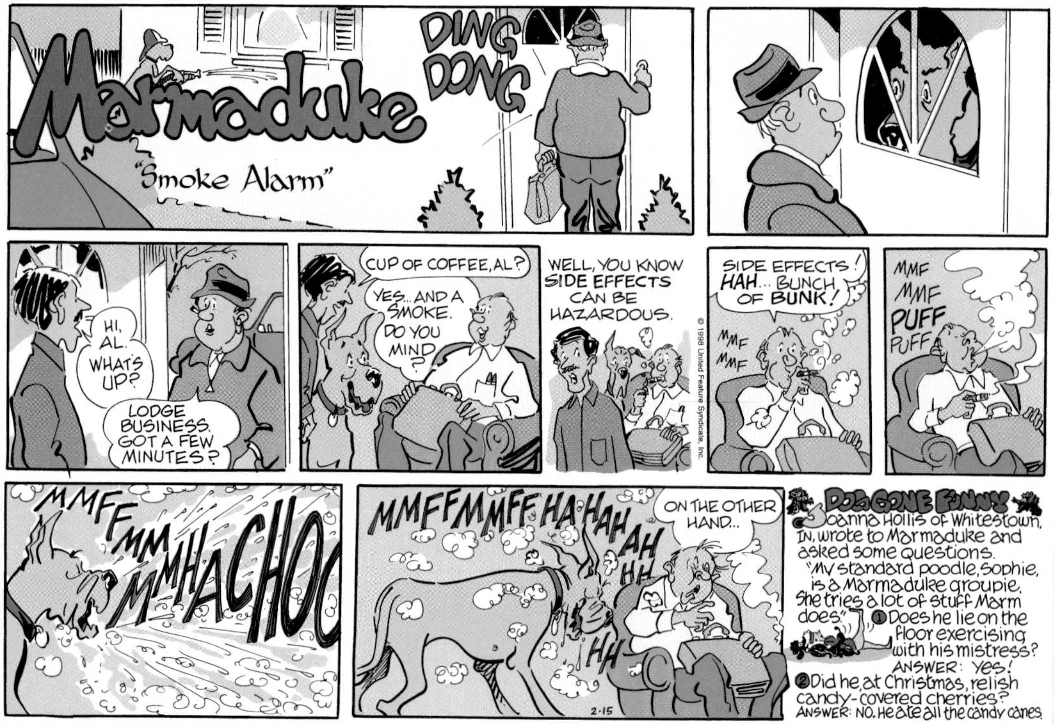
Marmaduke
"Smoke Alarm"
DING DONG
HI, AL. WHAT'S UP?
LODGE BUSINESS. GOT A FEW MINUTES?
CUP OF COFFEE, AL?
YES... AND A SMOKE. DO YOU MIND?
WELL, YOU KNOW SIDE EFFECTS CAN BE HAZARDOUS.
© 1998 United Feature Syndicate, Inc.
MMF MMF
SIDE EFFECTS! HAH... BUNCH OF BUNK!
MMF MMF PUFF PUFF
MMFF MM MMH ACHOO
MMFF MMFF HA HA HA AH HH HH
ON THE OTHER HAND...
2·15
DOG GONE FUNNY
Joanna Hollis of Whitestown, IN, wrote to Marmaduke and asked some questions.
"My standard poodle, Sophie, is a Marmaduke groupie. She tries a lot of stuff Marm does."
1 Does he lie on the floor exercising with his mistress?
ANSWER: Yes!
2 Did he, at Christmas, relish candy-covered cherries?
ANSWER: No. He ate all the candy canes.

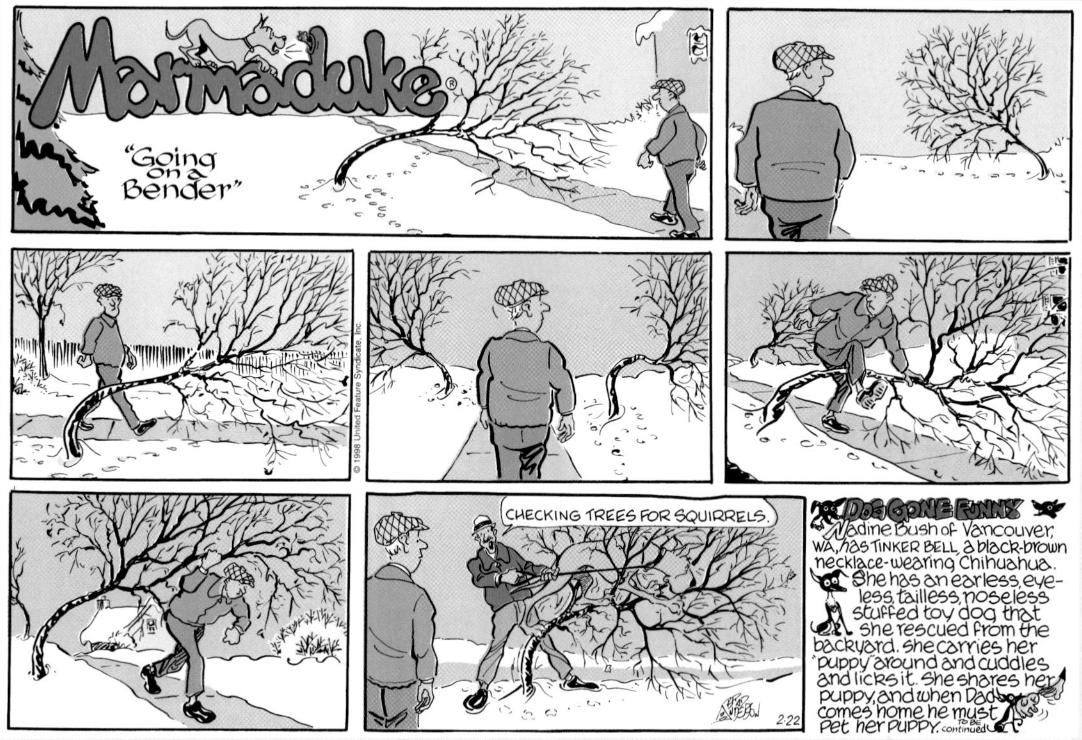
Marmaduke®
"Going on a Bender"
© 1998 United Feature Syndicate, Inc.
CHECKING TREES FOR SQUIRRELS.
2·22
DOG GONE FUNNY
Nadine Bush of Vancouver, WA, has TINKER BELL, a black-brown necklace-wearing Chihuahua.
She has an earless, eye-less, tailless, noseless stuffed toy dog that she rescued from the backyard. She carries her "puppy" around and cuddles and licks it. She shares her puppy, and when Dad comes home he must pet her PUPPY.
TO BE continued

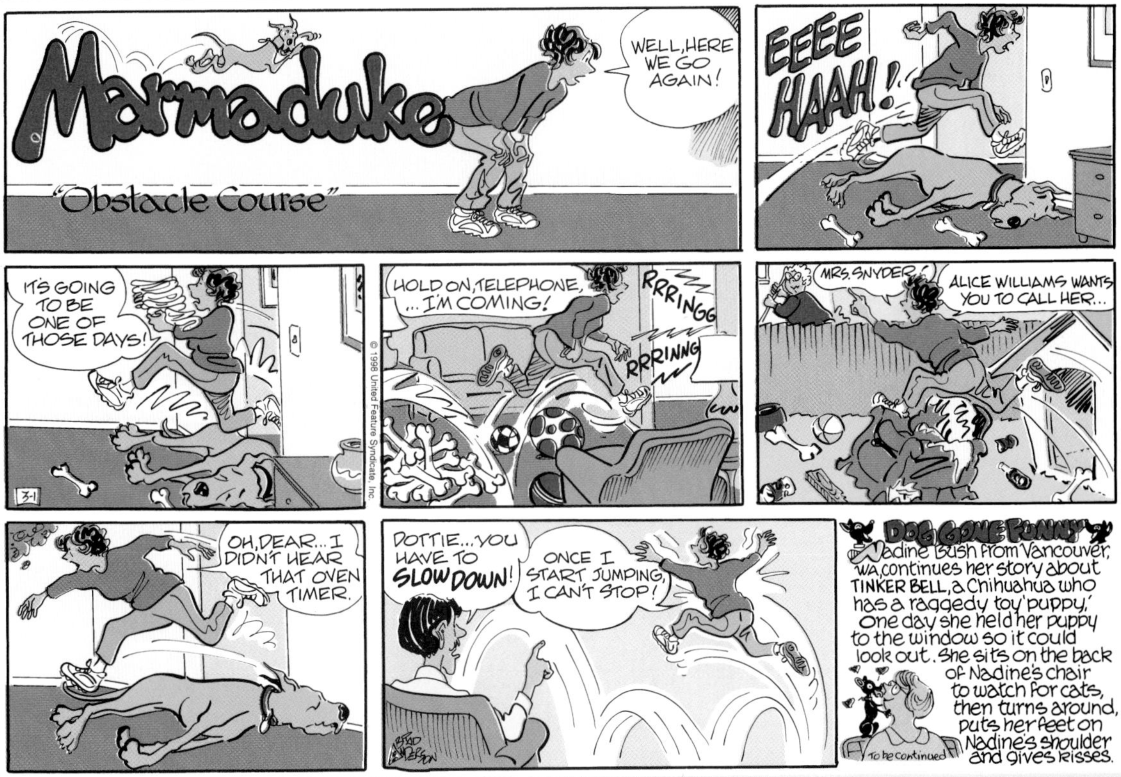
Marmaduke
"Obstacle Course"
WELL, HERE WE GO AGAIN!
EEEE HAAH!
IT'S GOING TO BE ONE OF THOSE DAYS!
3-1
© 1998 United Feature Syndicate, Inc.
HOLD ON, TELEPHONE, ... I'M COMING!
RRRINGG
RRRINNG
MRS. SNYDER!
ALICE WILLIAMS WANTS YOU TO CALL HER...
OH, DEAR... I DIDN'T HEAR THAT OVEN TIMER.
DOTTIE... YOU HAVE TO SLOW DOWN!
ONCE I START JUMPING, I CAN'T STOP!
BRAD ANDERSON
DOG GONE FUNNY
Nadine Bush from Vancouver, WA, continues her story about TINKER BELL, a Chihuahua who has a raggedy toy 'puppy.' One day she held her puppy to the window so it could look out. She sits on the back of Nadine's chair to watch for cats, then turns around, puts her feet on Nadine's shoulder and gives kisses.
To be continued

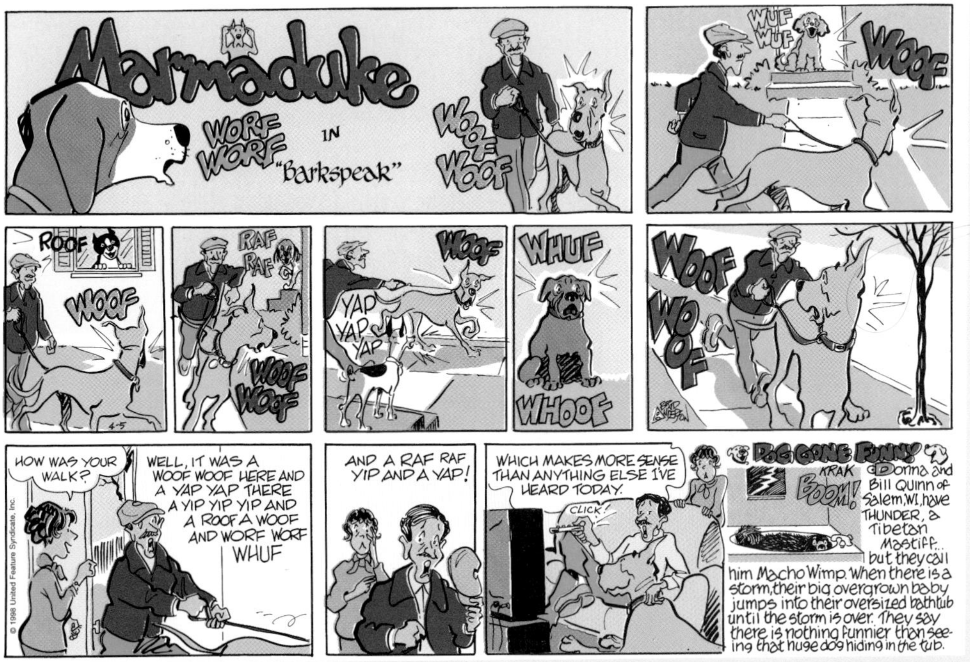
Marmaduke
WORF WORF
IN
"Barkspeak"
WOOF WOOF
WUF WUF
WOOF
ROOF
WOOF
4-5
RAF RAF
WOOF WOOF
WOOF
YAP YAP YAP
WHUF
WHOOF
WOOF WOOF
BRAD ANDERSON
© 1998 United Feature Syndicate, Inc.
HOW WAS YOUR WALK?
WELL, IT WAS A WOOF WOOF HERE AND A YAP YAP THERE A YIP YIP YIP AND A ROOF A WOOF AND WORF WORF WHUF
AND A RAF RAF YIP AND A YAP!
WHICH MAKES MORE SENSE THAN ANYTHING ELSE I'VE HEARD TODAY.
CLICK!
DOG GONE FUNNY
KRAK BOOM!
Donna and Bill Quinn of Salem, WI, have THUNDER, a Tibetan Mastiff... but they call him Macho Wimp. When there is a storm, their big overgrown baby jumps into their oversized bathtub until the storm is over. They say there is nothing funnier than seeing that huge dog hiding in the tub.

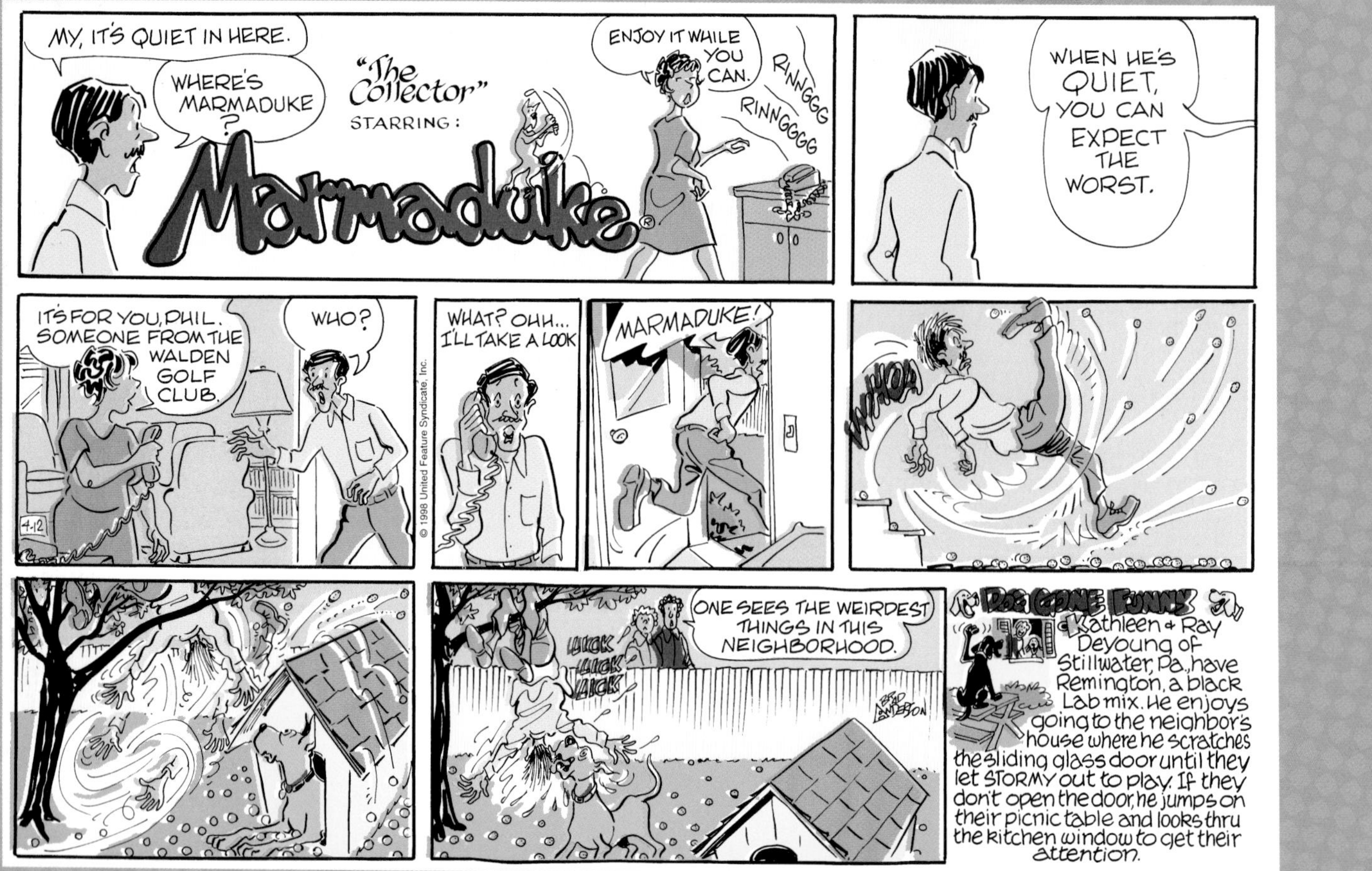

MY, IT'S QUIET IN HERE.
WHERE'S MARMADUKE ?
"The Collector" STARRING:
Marmaduke®
ENJOY IT WHILE YOU CAN.
RINNGGG
RINNGGGG
WHEN HE'S QUIET, YOU CAN EXPECT THE WORST.
IT'S FOR YOU, PHIL. SOMEONE FROM THE WALDEN GOLF CLUB.
WHO?
4-12
© 1998 United Feature Syndicate, Inc.
WHAT? OHH... I'LL TAKE A LOOK
MARMADUKE!
WHOA
LICK LICK LICK
ONE SEES THE WEIRDEST THINGS IN THIS NEIGHBORHOOD.
BRAD ANDERSON
DOG GONE FUNNY
Kathleen & Ray Deyoung of Stillwater, Pa., have Remington, a black Lab mix. He enjoys going to the neighbor's house where he scratches the sliding glass door until they let STORMY out to play. If they don't open the door, he jumps on their picnic table and looks thru the kitchen window to get their attention.

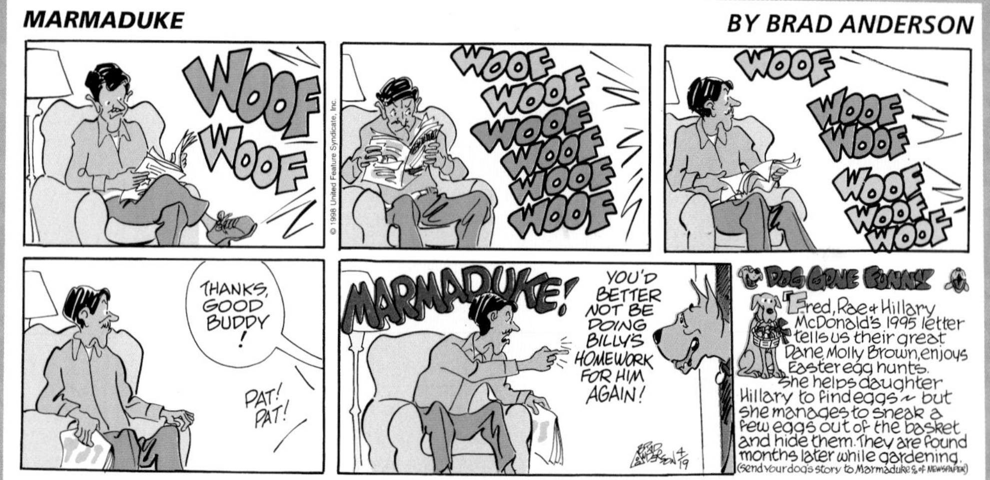

MARMADUKE
BY BRAD ANDERSON
WOOF WOOF
WOOF WOOF WOOF WOOF WOOF WOOF
© 1998 United Feature Syndicate, Inc.
WOOF WOOF WOOF WOOF WOOF WOOF
THANKS, GOOD BUDDY !
PAT! PAT!
MARMADUKE!
YOU'D BETTER NOT BE DOING BILLY'S HOMEWORK FOR HIM AGAIN!
BRAD ANDERSON 4-19
DOG GONE FUNNY
Fred, Rae & Hillary McDonald's 1995 letter tells us their great Dane Molly Brown, enjoys Easter egg hunts. She helps daughter Hillary to find eggs ~ but she manages to sneak a few eggs out of the basket and hide them. They are found months later while gardening.
(Send your dog's story to Marmaduke % of NEWSPAPER)

Marmaduke

"Couched demand"

RRUMMM

THUMP THUMP THUMP

TODAY'S LESSON... GET OFF THE COUCH BEFORE HE FLUFFS THE PILLOWS!

DOG GONE FUNNY
Lois Lynch of St Petersburg, FL, has Boone, a 10-year-old Beagle. Boone has a new friend... a CAT! The cat appears every morning and helps Boone eat his breakfast. Then he gives Boone several smooches. They sit on the porch for a while until the cat decides to head for home.

BRAD ANDERSON 4-26

OOPS!! SORRY, WRONG STRIP!

2000
Beyond
The Modern
of Marmaduk

and

d:

Times

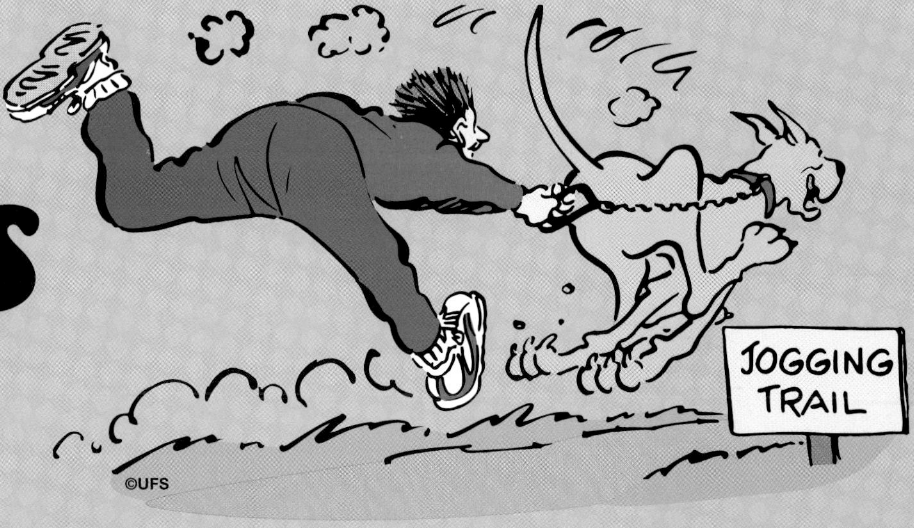

JOGGING TRAIL
©UFS

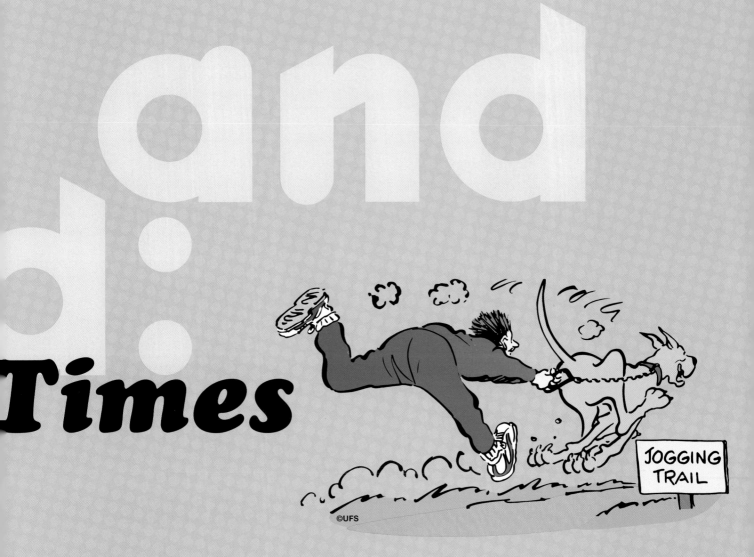

"An hour ago you were chewing on an old slipper.
Now you're a picky eater."

"Mints are missing from my purse.
Let me smell your breath."

"Yesterday I told him, 'No shoes,
no shirt, no service.'"

"I think he's trying to teach
you to shake hands."

"The good news is, he ate a good
nutritious meal. The bad news
is, it was yours."

"He could watch the power
windows all day."

"When did he get into leather?"

"Okay...I'll put some
frosting on your nose."

"No, it's not influenced by Picasso.
My model wouldn't stay still."

"Yes, they do look like the cushions off our couch."

Brad Anderson

Q: How did the *Marmaduke* strip get started? Where did you come up with that name?

A: I was a freelance magazine cartoonist. I had a contract with the *Saturday Evening Post* to provide them with ten cartoons each week, and they could pick from these for publication or reject them all. The late forties and early fifties were the Golden Age of cartoons. *The Saturday Evening Post*, *Collier's*, *The New Yorker*, and virtually all the major monthly magazines depended on cartoons. Magazines like *1000 Jokes* and *Judge* were primarily cartoon showcases. But television began to cut into magazine advertising starting in the fifties, and big magazines began to drop out. Seeing the writing on the wall, I started to submit strip ideas to various syndicates. Two small features were picked up. *Marmaduke* was offered a contract by National Newspaper Syndicate in 1953 and launched in 1954. It's been running ever since.

The name Marmaduke was once a common name in America, and it can still be found in phonebooks as a family name. It was also the name of a fictional character in a Revolutionary War–era book. It has an old-fashioned, slightly humorous ring to it—similar to what you find in other pet features that came later, like Heathcliff, Belvedere, and

I drew cartoons when I was a kid, first for my own amusement, then as a way of making extra spending money when I was a teenager.

Garfield. Marmaduke himself was modeled after a real dog—not a Great Dane, but a crazy boxer named Bruno who belonged to my stepfather.

Q: Did you always want to be a cartoonist? When did you start drawing cartoons?

A: I drew cartoons when I was a kid, first for my own amusement, then as a way of making extra spending money when I was a teenager. I sold my first cartoon at the age of fifteen. After serving in the Navy in World War II, I was accepted at Syracuse University; while there, I began selling cartoons to major magazines. That was the beginning of my cartoon career.

Q: How many papers does *Marmaduke* appear in now?

A: I'm not sure of the exact figure. Five hundred to six hundred at least, including papers in Europe, South America, Africa, and Australia. I get letters from all over the world!

Q: When you studied at Syracuse University's School of Fine Arts after your stint in World War II, what was the academic attitude toward cartooning? Was it tough for you to be taken seriously as an artist by your teachers there?

A: My professors at Syracuse were very encouraging, and I had no difficulty being taken seriously. In fact, quite a few notable cartoonists have come out of Syracuse, includ-ing Robb Armstrong (*Jump Start*) and the Pulitzer Prize–winning editorial cartoonist Jim Morin. So there's a rich tradition there, which I'm proud to have been a part of.

Q: I think a lot of people don't realize everything that goes into a cartoon. Many of us assume that the artist simply sits down at a table and tosses off a week's worth of work in an hour or so, then goes out to play golf!

A: A lot of new comic strips fail because the cartoonist, once he or she signs the contract, thinks they've got it made, and the hard part is over. Successful comics require dedicated work habits and fresh ideas. I follow the same routine each day. I get up early, go to the drawing board, and work on ideas or draw. This has always been my routine, going all the way back to my freelance days. I'm not much of a golfer—any free time I can squeeze in goes into working in my garden and traveling.

Q: I know that you are an admirer of the late Bill Mauldin's work. What made his cartoons so powerful? Did he influence you as an artist?

A: Mauldin wasn't really an influence; by the time I started seeing his stuff, I'd already developed my own style. But like many others, I admired the realism of his work...and the subject matter, of course: the life of the common soldier in World War II. Even though his cartoons were about the Army, and I served in the Navy, there was a lot I could relate to on a personal and artistic level. He was a master at communicating ideas through art and text.

Q: Who are some of the cartoonists that did influence you?

A: J. R. Williams (*Out Our Way*), Ted Key (*Hazel*), and Hank Ketcham (*Dennis the Menace*) were all influences, as was John Gallagher.

Q: What is more important in a panel or strip comic, the words or the art?

A: I try to balance words and art in *Marmaduke.* That doesn't mean the two have equal weight. The gagline complements the cartoon...or provides a surprise! *Marmaduke* leans heavily on action; *Marmaduke* cartoons are first and foremost visual. Think of the old Laurel and Hardy movies; they began as silent comedy, doing everything through action. Later, when talkies came in, dialogue became a part of their comedy, but the visual stuff was always there.

Q: When you sit down at the drawing board, are you concentrating more on telling a story or telling a joke?

A: I concentrate on creating a funny situation. Most newspapers detail the negative aspects of the world we live in. A lot of strips today are more interested in being politically correct and educating their readers than they are in entertaining them. *Marmaduke* allows readers to escape the front page and brings relief from the negativities in today's news.

Q: How did the "Dog Gone Funny" section of the strip get started?

A: I introduced "Dog Gone Funny" in the seventies. It came about as a result of all the

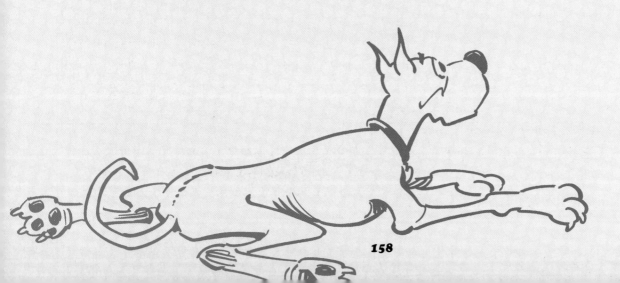

158

I concentrate on creating a funny situation.

letters I received from readers about their dogs. I would get, and I still get, a lot of mail from my readers—sometimes hundreds of letters a month. I tried to drop "Dog Gone Funny" once, but the readers protested too much!

Q: "Dog Gone Funny" is usually drawn in a different style than the *Marmaduke* panels. How do you decide what style is best suited to your material? Is it an instinctive choice, or do you consider a lot of things?

A: I try to portray not just the breed, but the character of the particular dog and the situation in a humorous way. That determines the style.

Q: How has *Marmaduke* evolved over the years?

A: All comics change if they last several years. *Marmaduke* evolved from a *Saturday Evening Post*–type cartoon to a more realistic cartoon that readers identified with, and I began to think of J. R. Williams's cartoonish-realism style.

Q: If, as is often said, an artist is only as good

as his tools, you must use some pretty good tools!

A: I use a Strathmore Bristol Board, 1-ply for the daily strips and 2-ply for the Sunday strips; a Windsor-Newton brush, Number 1, Series 7; and various pen points and permanent ink pens and markers. I currently use Koh-I-Noor permanent drawing ink.

Q: If you had to put your philosophy as a cartoonist into one sentence, what would it be?

A: Keep it simple, keep it funny, draw it well, and surprise the reader.

Q: What is the secret of *Marmaduke*'s success?

A: Thinking like a dog helps keep *Marmaduke* alive. Also, Marmaduke is a "real dog." He doesn't talk or walk on his hind legs.

Q: Unlike other famous cartoon animals, like Charles Schulz's Snoopy or Jim Davis's Garfield.

A: Right. Their animals are little cartoon people. Marmaduke is and always has been a cartoon dog.

Q: Is your supporting cast—the Winslow family—based on real people?

A: The Winslows were created as cartoon characters. Other characters in the strip were based on real people...but I'm not going to tell you who!

159

I don't do politics, religion, feminism, politically correct, any of that.

Q: How have the Winslows changed over the years? For example, did the feminist movement affect your depiction of Dottie Winslow?

A: I don't do politics, religion, feminism, politically correct, any of that. I leave that up to other comics and the news sections of the paper. Marmaduke is more interested in digging a hole. I do keep the strip current in terms of fashions, cars, et cetera, but none of that is central to the cartoons.

Q: Back in the 1980s, there was a TV show featuring Marmaduke and Heathcliff the cartoon cat. Are there new plans in the works for a return to TV—say, on the Cartoon Network?

A: Your guess is as good as mine. I don't have anything to do with that. It's all up to United Feature Syndicate, the company that owns and distributes *Marmaduke.*

Q: How do you keep *Marmaduke* fresh after fifty years?

A: *Marmaduke* stays fresh because the audience stays fresh. Kids follow it as they grow up into adulthood and old age. Then their own kids and grandkids follow it, so there's always a new audience.

Q: Any thoughts of retirement after fifty years?

A: Retiring? Yes—someday. Drawing a daily cartoon panel and strip is very confining. There are continuous daily deadlines. I have managed to survive without hiring assistants, but I'm grateful to my wife for taking over the business office, keeping records, filing, and contending with all the taxes: in short, for dealing with all the things that can make one wonder, Is all this aggravation worth it? Thanks to her, I've been able to concentrate on making a living and doing the thing I enjoy doing the most—drawing cartoons.